Laurence Sterne, George Saintsbury

The Letters, Sermons and Miscellaneous Writings of Laurence

Sterne

In Two Volumes. Vol. I

Laurence Sterne, George Saintsbury

The Letters, Sermons and Miscellaneous Writings of Laurence Sterne
In Two Volumes. Vol. I

ISBN/EAN: 9783744687706

Printed in Europe, USA, Canada, Australia, Japan

Cover: Foto ©Thomas Meinert / pixelio.de

More available books at **www.hansebooks.com**

Laurence Sterne.

THE LETTERS SERMONS and MISCELLANEOUS WRITINGS of LAURENCE STERNE

Edited by GEORGE SAINTSBURY
with
Illustrations by E. J. WHEELER

In two Volumes.
Volume the first.

LONDON 🌸 🌸 🌸 Published by
J. M. DENT & Co. Aldine House
69 Great Eastern Street, E.C.
MDCCCXCIV.

CONTENTS.

VOL. I.

vi

CONTENTS.

LIST OF ILLUSTRATIONS.

INTRODUCTION.

IT did not appear to be necessary, in the present edition of Sterne's novels, to include, or endeavour to include—for some of them are still copyright, and some unprinted—the whole of his miscellaneous works. The majority of the sermons are of extremely little interest. Of all the earlier ones, that given in *Tristram Shandy* itself is a fully sufficient example; and of the more deliberately Shandean discourses, printed in 1766 and later, those which have been selected here will, I think, satisfy the curiosity of most people. For the method, though obvious enough, and not particularly edifying, is also not extremely amusing in large doses.

The autobiographic fragment claimed a place of indisputable right; and the "History of a Good Warm Watch Coat," though not very much older than *Tristram Shandy* itself, *is* older; and in other points besides the selection of the name "Trim" is most interesting as a forerunner. Its usual companion in the last-century editions, the Rabelaisian scrap about Homenas, did not appear to me to possess sufficient interest to reappear. Respecting the letters themselves, I deliberated and pondered almost as much as Sir

Thomas Bertram himself (or Mr and Mrs Sterne, when they talked over their friends, Mr Blake and Miss Ash) could have thought proper, before finally determining what to do with them.   I decided at last to give all those included in the standard ten-volume edition of the *Works*, except the last four, which are, in that edition, admitted to be of dubious genuineness.   I may add, that the first three of these, while they are utterly uninteresting, appear to me to be almost certain *pastiches* by an imitator, and not a very clever imitator, of Sterne's style.   The "Impromptu" which, though not a letter at all, figures last in the *Letters* as usually printed, is a *coq-à-l'âne*, which Sterne might have written when he was, as its unknown godfather says, "soused," though we do not know that to be in this condition was a frequent vice of his.   The conclusion, however, in which, on the evident pattern of the conclusions of the two novels, a coarse line of Rochester's is dragged in to achieve a double meaning, is extremely suspicious. In these moods of his, Sterne usually went to originals less generally known than Rochester.

    The exclusion of these apocrypha has the additional advantage, that the collection now concludes, as it should, with the famous deathbed letter, of which even Thackeray acknowledged the force and pathos; while it enables me to say that nothing not certainly Sterne's is included here except those letters to him, which complete his correspondence.   Nor have I thought it necessary to exclude the "very sad dog-Latin" epistle, which, by the way, I am as nearly certain as if I had seen it written, is years older than the date usually assigned to it.   Mr Traill (who does not pronounce on the date of the letter) is of course absolutely correct in pointing out that Mr Fitzgerald has mistaken the application of the *quadraginta annos et plus*, of the conpleted *octavum lustrum*, in giving it to Sterne instead of Stevenson. But in 1767, the usually given date, Stevenson was close upon fifty (he was born in 1718), and the words would have been totally inapplicable to him. On the other hand, taking them literally would put the letter about 1758 or 1759, when the great fermentation which produced *Tristram* and changed Sterne's whole life took place, when the Fourmentelle flame was just a-kindling, and when other things (which would be absurd in 1767) suit well enough. Couched as it is in the blessed obscurity of a learned language, it cannot be intelligible except to those who are already initiated in that *Romana simplicitas* of speech to which we give a grosser name than simplicity, and of which they have " seen many others " in Latin literature itself.

The only other known documents attributed to Sterne, and not certainly falsehoods or forgeries, are the curious fragment which my friend M. Stapfer published, but which nothing but tradition attributes to our author, and which I do not myself believe to be his, and the various letters which have been published at different times, or which are still in MS.

A complete collection of all Sterne's letters, published and unpublished, would be by no means uninteresting ; but it would be quite alien from the plan of this edition, inasmuch as it would require not only the good-will of the owners of copyrights or of originals, but also an elaborate *apparatus criticus* in the arrangement and annotation of the correspondence. I had, however, for a time debated with myself whether it might be desirable to add a few from different sources; but I finally decided that to travel out of the limits of the standard edition, without giving a complete new one, would be inconvenient in many ways, not to mention that the intrinsic interest of the letters printed in this century is by no means great. One from Sterne to Warburton, printed some thirty years ago, and forming part of the correspondence already published, and re-printed here, is chiefly noticeable because of the half apologetic, half defiant tone of it ("I will, however, do my best; but laugh, my lord, I will, and as loud as I can too"), and for the audacious assertion, either equivocal or unintelligible, that the writer had "for nineteen years totally interrupted all correspondence with" Hall Stevenson, and had forgotten his hand.

The extra letters to this same Hall Stevenson, of which there are one or two, are no gain in any way. There remain the Fourmentelle and Blake correspon-dences, the former published many years ago by Mr John Murray for the Philobiblon Society, the latter printed for the first time by Mr Fitzgerald, who also gave some to the Archbishop of York, and refers to others. Messrs Murray have already allowed the first to be more than once reprinted; and I do not doubt that Mr Fitzgerald, whose literary courtesy is well known, would have allowed me to reprint the second. But neither seemed to me to be necessary. The Fourmentelle correspondence is no doubt genuine, though the story furnished with it to Mr Murray by Mrs Weston, the lady who sold him the letters, and represented herself as a friend of Miss Fourmen-

telle's, is a tissue of wild inaccuracies, to use no
stronger word. It seems, however, that Catherine
Beranger de Fourmentelle was a real person, who lived
at York with her mother just at the time of the appearance
of *Tristram*, came to London while Sterne was himself
living there to receive the fruits of his labours, and was
addressed by him, both at York and in town, in a series
of letters of extreme warmth, several interviews also
passing between them. Although " warm," however,
and doubtless not " proper" from a married man to
an unmarried girl, these letters contain nothing of
Sterne's usual double meaning, and none of the nauseous
sentimentalism of the " Eliza" series. The sentence
in them which has caused much hubbub, " God will
open a door when we shall sometime be much more
together, and enjoy our desires without fear of inter-
ruption," and which has been construed into a prophecy
of, or aspiration for, Mrs Sterne's death, need not
necessarily bear any such meaning. For the rest, the
letters are ordinary love-letters enough; and the bio-
graphical details, though they sometimes confirm other
sources of information, tell us little new. Nor can I
see anything so very curious in the letter written by
Sterne, but apparently intended for his " dear, dear
Kitty" to copy, and recommending *Tristram Shandy*
to some third person. Sterne was not a man of
Quixotic delicacy, and the supposed writer of the letter
is made quite honestly to admit that the author is a
great friend of hers, and that she is trying to do him
a service. As for the Blake series, it is addressed
to one of Sterne's colleagues in the Chapter at York,
who apparently had a difficult course of true love with

a Miss Ash, and for whom Sterne and Mrs Sterne did friendly offices. They exhibit the writer in a pleasant, amiable, unaffected mood; they give some gossipping particulars, and they show that Mr and Mrs Sterne could play up to each other in ordinary social life quite properly. But they cannot be said to be of great importance, or even of much interest.

Thus the probable reader will have in these two volumes all Sterne's work, outside the two novels which he has already had, that is really worth his attention. The Sterne shown here, whether in sermon, in fragment, or in epistle, will be little different from the Sterne in the two novels, for we have had few men of letters who were more of a piece than this singular parson. On the letters, it is hardly necessary to add anything to what has been said here and in the general introduction. Something must, but perhaps not much need, be said in the way of purely literary criticism of the contents of this volume. The matter of the *Letters* is avowedly more interesting than the manner. In the *Sermons*, the case is reversed. It has been supposed that in the less questionable characteristics of his epistolary style to women Sterne was imitating Swift, but I do not think this a necessary supposition. There is a certain manner which is common to almost all men of letters and brains when they address the other sex, a manner which, with individual alterations, is observable in the most different cases—in Swift and Scott, in Sterne and Sydney Smith. It is not exactly a case of

ὁ θὴρ δ' ἔβαινε δειλῶς
φοβεῖτο γὰρ Κυθήρην

as the poet has it. But "the beast" endeavours to subdue his worldly wit, and make it pleasant by jesting, to pay his court gallantly, and at the same time not servilely. Sterne is not the best example of this *commerce badinant*, as the Frenchman of his own time would have called it, but he is not the worst. In his general letters effect is evidently not aimed at, and it may be noted that in them his spelling is queer beyond the wont of men of his day.

The *Sermons*, on the other hand, especially the first instalment (which extends to Sermon XIV.), are the most carefully written things of his that we have in form, and show that slipshod writing was by no means necessary to him. Until he came deliberately to wear his cap and bells in the pulpit—the famous "That I deny," in the second Sermon, is a doubtful exception —there is not so very much difference, though undoubtedly there is some, between him and the usual divines of his own day and the day before, since Tillotson, a century earlier, had set the fashion of elegant and unscholastic writing. Nor do I think it in the very least necessary to suppose any conscious hypocrisy in Sterne even after he began, as in the later examples given here, to try experiments, to see how far Tristram in bands and gown could borrow the merits of Tristram in coat and *solitaire.* He could never here, any more than elsewhere, have arrived at the heights and depths of thought, religious or other ; and a curious example of it is the exceedingly commonplace turn which, after a not unpromising beginning, he gives to so great a text as that about Time and Chance. But though he could no more have preached

Catholic doctrine than he could have felt Evangelical fervour, he maintains both a fair standard of orthodoxy and a fair standard of morality even at his raciest, while, as already stated, he paid the pulpit the compliment of attending far more carefully to the minutiæ of composition than he ever did out of that rostrum.

His critics have not, I think, always kept in sight quite clearly enough the fact that in the known, or presumed, contents of the library of "Crazy Castle" Sterne must have found examples of this as well as of the other style of composition to which he addicted himself. He had found the lay *fatrasie* of the French fifteenth and sixteenth centuries popular, and he seems to have thought that the clerical *fatrasie* might likewise "draw." He could not indeed follow Maillard, Menot, Raulin, and their fellows quite as easily as he had followed Rabelais and Beroalde; but he did his best. And in this particular respect I please myself with thinking that he did much better than he would have done in our day, though in our day perhaps he would have found his vein even more profitable and popular. We hold our fans up at the eighteenth century for its want of propriety, but at least it did not often favour a greatly excessive sentimentality in the pulpit, which we can hardly say of ourselves. It left Sterne a prebendary; and it hanged Dodd. At the present day, Sterne no doubt would have had to make fewer jokes. But by burdening his energies with some slight deflection towards the glorification of the working man, by crying up the "living wage" (how beautifully he would have done it), and by making the simple exchange (*si peu que rien*) of "purity" for "impurity" as a favourite subject, I think he would have had not the slightest difficulty in arriving at canonries and archdeaconries, nor much in achieving deaneries or even bishoprics. I like him better as a mere prebendary, and as a little more than a mere novelist.

And in these capacities we may like him very much. He was not exactly a good man, though there have been many worse; and he was not exactly a great man, though there have been very few who so narrowly missed greatness. But he was, which many good and some great men have not been, a " rare man "—a man of altogether peculiar idiosyncrasy and distinction. He has been accused of histrionics; and it is true that there are very few, if any, writers of his merit who so constantly suggest the mask and the sock, the part and the cue. But if he was an actor rather than a creator, then we can give him the quality of greatness freely, for so great an actor is nowhere to be found in literature.

MEMOIRS

OF THE

LIFE AND FAMILY

OF THE LATE

REV. MR LAURENCE STERNE.

WRITTEN BY HIMSELF.

ROGER STERNE,* (grandson to Archbishop Sterne) Lieutenant in Handaside's regiment, was married to Agnes Hebert, widow of a captain of a good family: her family name was (I believe) Nuttle——though, upon recollection, that was the name of her father-in-law, who was a noted sutler in Flanders, in Queen Ann's wars, where my father married his wife's daughter (N.B. he was in debt to him) which was in September 25, 1711, Old Style.— This Nuttle had a son by my grandmother—a fine person of a man, but a graceless whelp—what became of him I know not.—The family (if any left), live now at Clonmel in the south of Ireland, at which town

---

* Mr Sterne was descended from a family of that name in Suffolk, one of which settled in Nottinghamshire. The following

I was born November 24th, 1713, a few days after my mother arrived from Dunkirk.—My birth-day was ominous to my poor father, who was, the day after our arrival, with many other brave officers broke, and sent adrift into the wide world with a wife and two children —the elder of which was Mary ; she was born at Lisle in French Flanders, July the tenth, one thousand seven hundred and twelve, New-Style.—This child was most unfortunate—she married one Weemans in Dublin—who used her most unmercifully—spent his substance, became a bankrupt, and left my poor sister to shift for herself,—which she was able to do but for a few months, for she went to a friend's house in the country, and died of a broken heart. She was a most beautiful woman—of a fine figure, and deserved a better

Genealogy is extracted from Thoresby's *Ducatus Leodinensis*, p. 215.

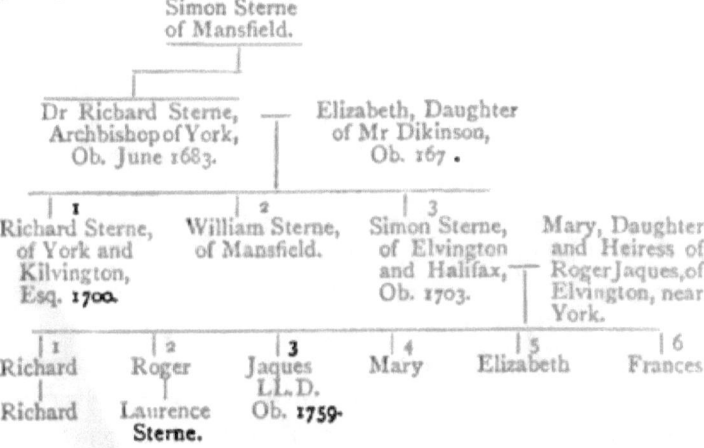

The arms of the family, says Guillam, in his Book of Heraldry, p. 77, are, Or, a chevron between three crosses flory, sable. The crest, on a wreath of his colours *a starling* proper.

Trifling circumstances are worthy of notice when connected with distinguished characters. The arms of Mr Sterne's family are no otherwise important than on account of the crest having afforded a hint for one of the finest stories in *The Sentimental Journey*. See vol. iv. of the present edition, p. 81.

fate.——The regiment, in which my father served, being broke, he left Ireland as soon as I was able to be carried, with the rest of his family, and came to the family seat at Elvington, near York, where his mother lived.   She was daughter to Sir Roger Jaques, and an heiress.   There we sojourned for about ten months, when the regiment was established, and our household decamped with bag and baggage for Dublin——within a month of our arrival, my father left us, being ordered to Exeter, where, in a sad winter, my mother and her two children followed him, travelling from Liverpool by land to Plymouth. (Melancholy description of this journey not necessary to be transmitted here.)   In twelve months we were all sent back to Dublin.—My mother, with three of us, (for she laid in at Plymouth of a boy, Joram), took ship at Bristol, for Ireland, and had a narrow escape from being cast away by a leak springing up in the vessel.—At length, after many perils, and struggles, we got to Dublin.—There my father took a large house, furnished it, and in a year and a half's time spent a great deal of money.——In the year one thousand seven hundred and nineteen, all unhinged again; the regiment was ordered, with many others, to the Isle of Wight, in order to embark for Spain in the Vigo expedition.   We accompanied the regiment, and were driven into Milford Haven, but landed at Bristol, from thence by land to Plymouth again, and to the Isle of Wight—where I remember we stayed encamped some time before the embarkation of the troops — (in this expedition from Bristol to Hampshire we lost poor Joram— a pretty boy, four years old, of the small-pox), my mother, sister, and myself, remained at the Isle of Wight during the Vigo expedition, and until the regiment had got back to Wicklow in Ireland, from whence my father sent for us.—We had poor Joram's

loss supplied during our stay in the Isle of Wight, by
the birth of a girl, Anne, born September the twenty-
third, one thousand seven hundred and nineteen.—This
pretty blossom fell at the age of three years, in the
barracks of Dublin—she was, as I well remember, of
a fine delicate frame, not made to last long, as were
most of my father's babes.—We embarked for Dublin,
and had all been cast away by a most violent storm ;
but through the intercessions of my mother, the captain
was prevailed upon to turn back into Wales, where we
stayed a month, and at length got into Dublin, and
travelled by land to Wicklow, where my father had for
some weeks given us over for lost.—We lived in the
barracks at Wicklow, one year, (one thousand seven
hundred and twenty) when Devijeher (so called after
Colonel Devijeher), was born ; from thence we decamped to stay half a year with Mr Fetherston, a
clergyman, about seven miles from Wicklow, who
being a relation of my mother's, invited us to his
parsonage at Animo.—It was in this parish, during our
stay, that I had that wonderful escape in falling through
a mill-race whilst the mill was going, and of being
taken up unhurt—the story is incredible, but known
for truth in all that part of Ireland—where hundreds
of the common people flocked to see me.—From hence
we followed the regiment to Dublin, where we lay in
the barracks a year.—In this year, one thousand seven
hundred and twenty-one, I learned to write, &c.—The
regiment ordered in twenty-two, to Carrickfergus in
the north of Ireland ; we all decamped, but got no
further than Drogheda, thence ordered to Mullengar,
forty miles west, where by Providence we stumbled
upon a kind relation, a collateral descendant from
Archbishop Sterne, who took us all to his castle, and
kindly entertained us for a year—and sent us to the
regiment at Carrickfergus, loaded with kindnesses, &c.—

a most rueful and tedious journey had we all, in March, to Carrickfergus, where we arrived in six or seven days—little Devijeher here died, he was three years old—He had been left behind at nurse at a farm-house near Wicklow, but was fetch'd to us by my father the summer after—another child sent to fill his place, Susan; this babe too left us behind in this weary journey—The autumn of that year, or the spring afterwards, (I forget which) my father got leave of his colonel to fix me at school—which he did near Halifax, with an able master; with whom I stayed some time, 'till by God's care of me my cousin Sterne, of Elvington, became a father to me, and sent me to the university, &c. &c. To pursue the thread of our story, my father's regiment was the year after ordered to Londonderry, where another sister was brought forth, Catherine, still living, but most unhappily estranged from me by my uncle's wickedness, and her own folly—from this station the regiment was sent to defend Gibraltar, at the siege, where my father was run through the body by Captain Phillips, in a duel, (the quarrel began about a goose) with much difficulty he survived—though with an impaired constitution, which was not able to withstand the hardships it was put to—for he was sent to Jamaica, where he soon fell by the country fever, which took away his senses first, and made a child of him, and then, in a month or two, walking about continually without complaining, till the moment he sat down in an arm chair, and breathed his last—which was at Port Antonio, on the north of the island.—My father was a little smart man—active to the last degree, in all exercises—most patient of fatigue and disappointments, of which it pleased God to give him full measure—he was in his temper somewhat rapid and hasty—but of a kindly, sweet disposition, void of all design; and so innocent in his own intentions, that he suspected

no one ; **so that you** might have cheated him ten times
in a day, **if nine had** not been sufficient for your purpose
—my poor **father died in** March, 1731—I remained
at Halifax 'till **about** the **latter** end of that year, and
cannot omit mentioning this **anecdote of** myself, and
school-master——He had **had the ceiling** of the
school-room new white-washed—the ladder remained
there—I **one** unlucky day mounted it, and wrote with
a brush in large capital letters, LAU. STERNE, for
which **the** usher severely whipped me. **My** master
was very much hurt at this, and said, before me, that
never should that name be effaced, for I was a boy of
genius, and he **was sure** I should come to preferment—
this expression made **me** forget the stripes I had received
—In the year thirty-two * **my** cousin sent me to the
university, where I staid some **time.** 'Twas there that
I commenced a friendship **with Mr H . . .** which
has been **most** lasting on both **sides—I** then came
to York, **and** my uncle got me the living of Sutton
—and at **York** I became acquainted with your mother,
and courted her for **two** years—she owned she liked
me, but thought herself not rich enough, **or** me too
poor, to be joined together—she went **to** her sister's in
S——, and **I** wrote to her often—I believe then **she**
was partly determined to have me, but would not say
so—at her return she fell into a consumption—and one
evening that **I** was **sitting** by her with an almost
broken **heart to see her** so ill, she said, " My dear
Laurey, **I** can **never be** yours, for I verily believe I
have **not** long to live—but I have left you every
shilling **of** my fortune ; "—upon that she shewed me
her will—this generosity overpowered me.—It pleased

* He was admitted of Jesus College, **in** the university of
Cambridge, 6th July, 1733, under the tuition of Mr Cannon.
  Matriculated 29th March, 1735.
  Admitted to the degree of B.A. in January, 1736.
  ————M.A. at the Commencement, 1740.

God that she recovered, and I married her in the year 1741. My uncle * and myself were then upon very good terms, for he soon got me the Prebendary of York—but he quarrelled with me afterwards, because I would not write paragraphs in the news-papers—though he was a party-man, I was not, and detested such dirty work : thinking it beneath me—from that period, he † became my bitterest enemy.—By my wife's means I got the living of Stillington—a friend of her's in the south had promised her, that if she married a clergyman in Yorkshire, when the living became vacant, he would make her a compliment of it. I remained near twenty years at Sutton, doing duty at both places —I had then very good health.—Books, painting,‡ fiddling, and shooting were my amusements; as to the Squire of the parish, I cannot say we were upon a very friendly footing—but at Stillington, the family of the C——'s shewed us every kindness—'twas most truly agreeable to be within a mile and a half of an amiable family, who were ever cordial friends—In the year 1760, I took a house at York for your mother and yourself, and went up to London to publish § my two first volumes of Shandy.‖ In that year Lord

* Jaques Sterne, LL.D. He was Prebendary of Durham, Canon Residentiary, Precentor and Prebendary of York, Rector of Rise, and Rector of Hornsea cum Riston, both in the East Riding of the county of York. He died June 9, 1759.

† It hath however been insinuated, that he for some time wrote a periodical electioneering paper at York, in defence of the Whig interest. *Monthly Review*, vol. 53, p. 344.

‡ A specimen of Mr Sterne's abilities in the art of designing, may be seen in Mr Wodhul's poems, 8vo, 1772,

§ The first edition was printed in the preceding year at York.

‖ The following is the order in which Mr Sterne's publications appeared :

1747. The Case of Elijah and the Widow of Zerephath considered : A charity-sermon preached on Good Friday, April 17, 1747, for the support of two charity-schools in York.

1750. The Abuses of Conscience : Set forth in a sermon preached in the cathedral church of St Peter's, York, at the

Falconbridge presented me with the curacy of Coxwold—a sweet retirement in comparison of Sutton.
In sixty-two I went to France before the peace was
concluded, and you both followed me.—I left you
both in France, and in two years after I went to Italy
for the recovery of my health—and when I called
upon you, I tried to engage your mother to return to
England, with me—she * and yourself are at length
come—and I have had the inexpressible joy of seeing
my girl every thing I wished her.

*I have set down these particulars relating to my family,
and self, for my Lydia, in case hereafter she might have
a curiosity, or a kinder motive to know them.*

⁂

A S Mr Sterne, in the foregoing narrative, hath
brought down the account of himself until within
a few months of his death, it remains only to
mention that he left York about the end of the year
1767, and came to London in order to publish *The
Sentimental Journey*, which he had written during the
preceding summer at his favourite living of Coxwold.
His health had been for some time declining, but he

summer assizes, before the Hon. Mr Baron Clive, and the
Hon. Mr Baron Smythe, on Sunday, July 29, 1750.
  1759. Vol. 1 and 2, of Tristram Shandy.
  1760. Vol. 1 and 2, of Sermons.
  1761. Vol. 3 and 4, of Tristram Shandy.
  1762. Vol. 5 and 6, of Tristram Shandy.
  1765. Vol. 7 and 8, of Tristram Shandy.
  1766. Vol. 3 and 4, of Sermons.
  1767. Vol. 9, of Tristram Shandy.
  1768. The Sentimental Journey.
The remainder of his works were published after his death.
  * From this passage it appears that the present account of
Mr Sterne's Life and Family was written about six months
only before his death.

continued to visit his friends, and retained his usual flow of spirits. In February, 1768, he began to perceive the approaches of death, and with the concern of a good man, and the solicitude of an affectionate parent, devoted his attention to the future welfare of his daughter. His letters at this period reflect so much credit on his character, that it is to be lamented some others in the collection were permitted to see the light. After a short struggle with his disorder, his debilitated and worn-out frame submitted to fate on the 18th day of March 1768, at his lodgings in Bond-street. He was buried at the new burying-ground, belonging to the parish of St George, Hanover-square, on the 22d of the same month, in the most private manner; and hath since been indebted to strangers for a monument very unworthy of his memory; on which the following lines are inscribed.

> " Near to this Place
> Lies the Body of
> The Reverend Laurence Sterne, A.M.
> Died September 13th, 1768,*
> Aged 53 Years.
> ' *Ah! molliter ossa quiescant.*'

If a sound Head, warm Heart, and Breast humane,
Unsullied Worth, and Soul without a stain;
If mental Powers could ever justly claim
The well-won Tribute of immortal Fame,
Sterne was *the Man*, who with gigantic Stride,
Mowed down luxuriant Follies far and wide.
Yet what, though keenest Knowledge of Mankind
Unseal'd to him the Springs that move the Mind;

---

* It is scarcely necessary to observe that this date is erroneous.

What did it cost him? ridicul'd, abus'd,
By Fools insulted, and by Prudes accus'd.
In his, mild Reader, view thy future Fate,
Like him despise, what 'twere a Sin to hate.

This monumental stone was erected by two brother
masons; for although he did not live to be a member
of their society, yet as his all incomparable performances
evidently prove him to have acted by rule and square,
they rejoice in this opportunity of perpetuating his high
and irreproachable character to after ages.

W. & S."

LETTERS

OF THE LATE

LAURENCE STERNE

TO

HIS MOST INTIMATE FRIENDS.

TO

DAVID GARRICK, Esq.

WHEN I was asked to whom I should dedicate these Volumes, I carelessly answered, To no one—Why not? (replied the person who put the question to me.) Because most Dedications look like begging a protection to the book. Perhaps a worse interpretation may be given to it. No, no! already so much obliged, I cannot, will not, put another tax upon the generosity of any friend of Mr Sterne's, or mine. I went home to my lodgings, and gratitude warmed my heart to such a pitch, that I vowed they should be dedicated to the man my father so much admired—who, with an unprejudiced eye, read, and approved his works, and moreover loved the man— 'Tis to Mr Garrick then, that I dedicate these Genuine Letters.

Can I forget the sweet Epitaph * which proved Mr

---

* Shall Pride a heap of sculptur'd marble raise,
  Some worthless, unmourn'd, titled fool to praise
  And shall we not by one poor grave-stone learn
  Where Genius, Wit, and Humour, sleep with *Sterne?*
  D. G.

Mr Sterne was born at Clonmel, in Ireland, November 24, 1713; and died, in London, March 18 1768.

Garrick's friendship, and opinion of him? 'Twas a tribute to friendship—and as a tribute of my gratitude I dedicate these Volumes to a man of understanding and feeling—Receive this, as it is meant—May you, dear Sir, approve of these Letters, as much as Mr Sterne admired you—but Mr Garrick, with all his urbanity, can never carry the point half so far, for Mr Sterne was an enthusiast, if it is possible to be one, in favour of Mr Garrick.

This may appear a very simple Dedication, but Mr Garrick will judge by his own sensibility, that I can feel more than I can express, and I believe he will give me credit for all my grateful acknowledgments.

I am, with every sentiment of gratitude and esteem,

Dear Sir,

Your obliged

humble Servant,

LYDIA STERNE DE MEDALLE.

London,
 June, 1775.

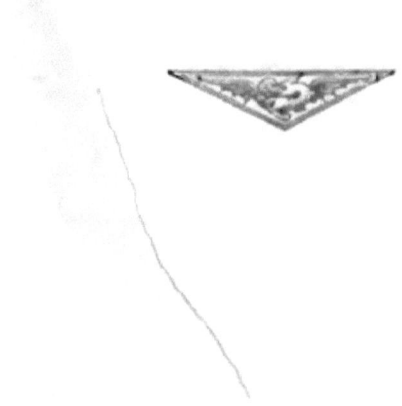

PREFACE.

IN publishing these Letters the Editor does but comply with her mother's request, which was, that if any Letters were publish'd under Mr Sterne's name, those she had in her possession (as well as those that her father's friends would be kind enough to send to her) should be likewise publish'd—She depends much on the candour of the Public for the favourable reception of them,——their being genuine,* she thinks, and hopes, will render them not unacceptable—She has already experienced much benevolence and generosity from her late father's friends—the remembrance of which will ever warm her heart with gratitude!

* Besides the Letters printed by Mrs Medalle, those written by Mr Sterne to Eliza, and a few others, are added to the present Edition. (*Original Note.*)

IN MEMORY OF

MR STERNE,

AUTHOR OF THE

SENTIMENTAL JOURNEY.

WITH wit, and genuine humour, to dispel,
    From the desponding bosom, gloomy care,
    And bid the gushing tear, at the sad tale
Of hapless love or filial grief to flow
From the full sympathising heart, were thine;
These powers, O STERNE! but now thy fate demands
(No plumage nodding o'er the emblazon'd hearse
Proclaiming honour where no virtue shone)
But the sad tribute of a heart-felt sigh:
What tho' no taper cast its deadly ray,
Nor the full choir sing requiems o'er thy tomb,
The humbler grief of friendship is not mute;
And poor Maria, with her faithful kid,
Her auburn tresses carelessly entwin'd
With olive foliage, at the close of day,
Shall chant her plaintive vespers at thy grave.

Thy shade too, gentle Monk, 'mid awful night,
Shall pour libations from its friendly eye ;
For erst his sweet benevolence bestow'd
Its generous pity, and bedew'd with tears
The sod, which rested on thy aged breast.

CHARACTER AND EULOGIUM

OF

STERNE AND HIS WRITINGS;

IN A

FAMILIAR EPISTLE FROM A GENTLEMAN IN
IRELAND TO HIS FRIEND.

[Written in the Year 1769.]

WHAT trifle comes next?—Spare the censure,
  my friend,
  This letter's no more from beginning to end:
Yet, when you consider (your laughter, pray, stifle)
The advantage, the importance, the use of a trifle—
When you think too beside—and there's nothing
  more clear—
That pence compose millions, and moments the year,
You surely will grant me, nor think that I jest,
That life's but a series of trifles at best.

How wildly digressive! yet could I, O STERNE,*
Digress with thy skill, with thy freedom return!
The vain wish I repress—Poor YORICK! no more
Shall thy mirth and thy jest " set the table on a
  roar ; "
No more thy sad tale, with simplicity told,
O'er each feeling breast its strong influence hold,
From the wise and the brave call forth sympathy's sigh,
Or swell with sweet anguish humanity's eye :
Here and there in a page if a blemish appear,

---

* The late reverend *Laurence Sterne*, A.M., &c., author of
that truly original, humorous, heteroclite work, called, The
Life and Opinions of *Tristram Shandy*, of A Sentimental Journey through France and Italy (which, alas! he did not live
to finish), and of some volumes of Sermons. Of his skill in
delineating and supporting his characters, those of the father
of his hero, of his uncle *Toby*, and of corporal *Trim* (out of
numberless others), afford ample proof: To his power in the
pathetic, whoever shall read the stories of *Le Fevre*, *Maria*,
the Monk, and *the Dead Ass*, must, if he has feelings, bear sufficient testimony ; and his *Sermons* throughout (though sometimes, perhaps, chargeable with a levity not entirely becoming
the pulpit) breathe the kindest spirit of *Philanthropy*, of *good-
will towards man*.   For the few exceptional parts of his works,
those small blemishes

> *Quas aut incuria fudit*
> *Aut humana parum cavit natura—*

suffer them, kind critic, to rest with his ashes !

The above eulogium will, I doubt not, appear to you (and
perhaps also to many others) much too high for the literary
character of STERNE ; I have not at present either leisure or
inclination to enter into argument upon the question ; but, in
truth, I consider myself as largely his debtor for the tears and
the laughter he so frequently excited, and was desirous to leave
behind me (for so long at least as this trifle shall remain) some
small memorial of my gratitude : I will even add, that, although
I regard the memory of *Shakespeare* with a veneration little
short of idolatry, I esteem the *Monk's horn-box* a relick " as
devoutly to be wished," as a pipe-stopper, a walking stick, or
even an ink-stand of the *mulberry-tree*.

(And what page, or what life, from a blemish is
    clear ?)
T<small>RIM</small> and T<small>OBY</small> with soft intercession attend ;
L<small>E</small> F<small>EVRE</small> intreats you to pardon his friend ;
M<small>ARIA</small> too pleads for her fav'rite distress'd,
As you feel for her sorrows, O grant her request !
Should these advocates fail, I've another to call,
One tear of his M<small>ONK</small> shall obliterate all.
Favour'd pupil of Nature and Fancy, of yore,
Whom from Humour's embrace sweet Philanthropy
    bore,
While the Graces and Loves scatter flowers on thy
    urn,
And Wit weeps the blossom too hastily torn ;
This meed too, kind Spirit, unoffended receive
From a youth next to S<small>HAKESPEARE</small>'s who honours
    thy grave !

LETTERS.

Letter i.*

To Miss L——.

YES! I will steal from the world, and not a babbling tongue shall tell where I am—Echo shall not so much as whisper my hiding-place —suffer thy imagination to paint it as a little sun-gilt cottage, on the side of a romantic hill—dost thou think I will leave love and friendship behind me? No! they shall be my companions in solitude, for they will sit down and rise up with me in the amiable form of my L.—We will be as merry and as innocent as our first parents in Paradise, before the arch fiend entered that undescribable scene.

The kindest affections will have room to shoot and expand in our retirement, and produce such fruit as madness, and envy, and ambition have always killed in the bud.—Let the human tempest and hurricane rage at a distance, the desolation is beyond the horizon of peace.—My L. has seen a Polyanthus blow in

* This and the three subsequent Letters were written by Mr Sterne to his wife, while she resided in Staffordshire, before their marriage.

December—some friendly wall has sheltered it from the biting wind.—No planetary influence shall reach us, but that which presides and cherishes the sweetest flowers.—God preserve us! how delightful this prospect in idea! We will build, and we will plant, in our own way—simplicity shall not be tortured by art—we will learn of nature how to live—she shall be our alchymist, to mingle all the good of life into one salubrious draught.—The gloomy family of care and distrust shall be banished from our dwelling, guarded by thy kind and tutelar deity—we will sing our choral songs of gratitude, and rejoice to the end of our pilgrimage.

Adieu, my L. Return to one who languishes for thy society.

L. STERNE.

Letter ij.

To the same.

You bid me tell you, my dear L., how I bore your departure for S——, and whether the valley where D'Estella stands, retains still its looks—or, if I think the roses or jessamines smell as sweet, as when you left it—Alas! every thing has now lost its relish and look! The hour you left D'Estella, I took to my bed.—I was worn out with fevers of all kinds, but most by that fever of the heart with which thou knowest well I have been wasting these two years—and shall continue wasting till you quit S——. The good Miss S——, from the forebodings of the best of hearts, thinking I was ill, insisted upon my going to her.—What can be the cause, my dear L., that I never have been able to see the face of this mutual friend, but I feel myself rent to pieces? She made me stay an hour with her, and in that short space I burst into tears a dozen different times—and in such affectionate gusts of passion, that she was constrained to leave the room, and sympathize in her dressing-room —I have been weeping for you both, said she, in a tone of the sweetest pity—for poor L.'s heart, I have long known it—her anguish is as sharp as yours—her heart as tender—her constancy as great—her virtues as heroic—Heaven brought you not together to be tormented. I could only answer her with a kind look, and a heavy sigh—and returned home to your lodgings (which I have hired till your return) to resign myself to misery—Fanny had prepared me a supper—she is all attention to me—but I sat over it with tears; a bitter sauce, my L., but I could eat it with no other— for the moment she began to spread my little table, my heart fainted within me.—One solitary plate, one knife, one fork, one glass!—I gave a thousand pensive, penetrating looks at the chair thou hadst so often graced, in those quiet and sentimental repasts—then laid down my knife and fork, and took out my handkerchief, and clapped it across my face, and wept like a child.—I do so this very moment, my L.; for, as I take up my pen, my poor pulse quickens, my pale face glows, and tears are trickling down upon the paper, as I trace the word L——. O thou! blessed in thyself, and in thy virtues—blessed to all that know thee—to me most so, because more do I know of thee than all thy sex.— This is the philtre, my L., by which thou hast charmed me, and by which thou wilt hold me thine, whilst virtue and faith hold this world together.—This, my friend, is the plain and simple magic, by which I told Miss —— I have won a place in that heart of thine, on which I depend so satisfied, that time, or distance, or change of every thing which might alarm the hearts of little men, create no uneasy suspense in mine—Wast thou to stay in S—— these seven years, thy friend, though he would grieve, scorns to doubt, or to be doubted—'tis the only exception where security is not the parent of danger.—I told you poor Fanny was all attention to me since your departure—contrives every day bringing in the name of L. She told me last night (upon giving me some hartshorn), she had observed my illness began the very day of your departure for S——; that I had never held up my head, had seldom, or scarce ever, smiled, had fled from all society—that she verily believed I was broken-hearted, for she had never entered the room, or passed by the door, but she heard me sigh heavily—that I neither eat, or slept, or took pleasure in any thing as before;—judge then, my L., can the valley look so well—or the roses and jessamines smell so sweet as heretofore? Ah me!—but adieu—the vesper bell calls me from thee to my God!

L. STERNE.

Letter iij.

To the same.

BEFORE now my L. has lodged an indictment against me in the high court of Friendship—I plead guilty to the charge, and intirely submit to the mercy of that amiable tribunal.—Let this mitigate my punishment, if it will not expiate my transgression—do not say that I shall offend again in the same manner, though a too easy pardon sometimes occasions a repetition of the same fault.—A Miser says, though I do no good with my money to-day, to-morrow shall be marked with some deed of beneficence.—The Libertine says, let me enjoy this week in forbidden and luxurious pleasures, and the next I will dedicate to serious thought and reflection.—The Gamester says, let me have one more chance with the dice, and I will never touch them more. —The Knave of every profession wishes to obtain but independency, and he will become an honest man.—The Female Coquette triumphs in tormenting her inamorato, for fear, after marriage, he should not pity her.

The apparition of the fifth instant (for letters may almost be called so) proved more welcome as I did not expect it. Oh! my L——, thou art kind indeed to make an apology for me, and thou never wilt assuredly repent of one act of kindness—for being thy debtor, I will pay thee with interest.—Why does my L. complain of the desertion of friends?—Where does the human being live that will not join in this complaint? —It is a common observation, and perhaps too true, that married people seldom extend their regards beyond their own fire-side.—There is such a thing as parsimony in esteem, as well as money—yet as one costs nothing, it might be bestowed with more liberality.—We cannot gather grapes from thorns, so we must not expect kind attachments from persons who are wholly folded up in selfish schemes. I do not know whether I most despise, or pity such characters—nature never made an unkind creature—ill usage, and bad habits, have deformed a fair and lovely creation.

My L.!—thou art surrounded by all the melancholy gloom of winter; wert thou alone, the retirement would be agreeable.——Disappointed ambition might envy such a retreat, and disappointed love would seek it out.—Crowded towns, and busy societies, may delight the unthinking and the gay—but solitude is the best nurse of wisdom.—Methinks I see my contemplative girl now in the garden, watching the gradual approaches of spring.—Dost not thou mark with delight the first vernal buds? the snow-drop, and primrose, these early and welcome visitors, spring beneath thy feet.—Flora and Pomona already consider thee as their handmaid; and in a little time will load thee with their sweetest blessing.—The feathered race are all thy own, and with them, untaught harmony will soon begin to cheer thy morning and evening walks.—Sweet as this may be, return—return—the birds of Yorkshire will tune their pipes, and sing as melodiously as those of Staffordshire.

Adieu, my beloved L., thine too much for my *peace*.

L. STERNE.

Letter iv.

To the same.

I HAVE offended her whom I so tenderly love!— what could tempt me to it! but if a beggar was to knock at thy gate, would thou not open the door and be melted with compassion?—I know thou wouldst, for Pity has erected a temple in thy bosom.—Sweetest, and best of all human passions! let thy web of tenderness cover the pensive form of affliction, and soften the darkest shades of misery! I have re-considered this apology, and, alas! what will it accomplish? Arguments, however finely spun, can never change the nature of things—very true—so a truce with them.

I have lost a very valuable friend by a sad accident, and what is worse, he has left a widow and five young children to lament this sudden stroke.—If real usefulness and integrity of heart could have secured him from this, his friends would not now be mourning his untimely fate—These dark and seemingly cruel dispensations of Providence, often make the best of human hearts complain.—Who can paint the distress of an affectionate mother, made a widow in a moment, weep-

ing in bitterness over a numerous, helpless, and father-
less offspring!—God! these are thy chastisements, and
require (hard task!) a pious acquiescence.

Forgive me this digression, and allow me to drop
a tear over a departed friend; and, what is more
excellent, an honest man. My L.! thou wilt feel
all that kindness can inspire in the death of——— The
event was sudden, and thy gentle spirit would be more
alarmed on that account.—But, my L., thou hast less to
lament, as old age was creeping on, and her period of
doing good, and being useful, was nearly over.—At
sixty years of age the tenement gets fast out of repair,
and the lodger with anxiety thinks of a discharge.—In
such a situation the poet might well say,

"The soul uneasy, etc."

My L. talks of leaving the country—may a kind
angel guide thy steps hither!—Solitude at length grows
tiresome.—Thou sayest thou wilt quit the place with
regret—I think so too.—Does not something uneasy
mingle with the very reflection of leaving it?—It is
like parting with an old friend, whose temper and
company one has long been acquainted with.—I think
I see you looking twenty times a day at the house—
almost counting every brick and pane of glass, and
telling them at the same time with a sigh, you are
going to leave them.—Oh happy modification of matter!
they will remain insensible of thy loss.—But how wilt
thou be able to part with thy garden?—The recollection of so many pleasing walks must have endeared it
to you. The trees, the shrubs, the flowers, which
thou reared with thy own hands—will they not droop
and fade away sooner upon thy departure?—Who will
be the successor to nurse them in thy absence?—
Thou wilt leave thy name upon the myrtle-tree.—
If trees, and shrubs, and flowers, could compose an

elegy, I should expect **a very** plaintive one upon this subject.

Adieu, **adieu!** Believe me ever, **ever** thine,

L. Sterne.

Letter v.

To Mrs F——.

York, Tuesday, Nov. 19, 1759.

Dear Madam,

Your kind enquiries after my health, deserve my best thanks.—What **can** give **one** more pleasure than the **good wishes of those** we value?—I am sorry you give **so bad** an account **of** your own health, **but** hope you will find benefit from tar-water—it **has** been of infinite service to me.—I suppose, my good **lad**y, by what you say in your letter, "that I am busy writing **an** extraordinary book," **that** your intelligence comes from York—the fountain-head of all chit-chat news—and —**no** matter.—Now **for** your desire of knowing the **reason of** my turning author? why truly I am tired of employing my brains for other people's advantage.— 'Tis a foolish sacrifice I have made for some years to an ungrateful person.—I depend much upon the candour of **the** publick, but I shall not pick out a jury **to** try the merit of my book amongst ********, and—till you read my Tristram, do not, like some people, condemn it.—Laugh I am sure you will at some passages. —I have hired a small house in **the** Minster Yard for **my** wife and daughter—the latter is to begin dancing, &c., **if** I cannot leave her a fortune, I will at least give her **an** education.——As I shall publish my works very soon, I shall **be in town** by March, and shall have **the** pleasure of meeting with you.——All your

friends are well, and ever hold you in the same estima-
tion that your sincere friend does.

Adieu, dear lady. Believe me, with every wish for
your happiness, your most faithful, &c.

LAURENCE STERNE.

Letter bi.

To Dr ******.

DEAR SIR,   Jan. 30, 1760.

—*De mortuis nil nisi bonum*, is a maxim which you
have so often of late urged in conversation, and in your
letters (but in your last especially), with such serious-
ness, and severity against me, as the supposed trans-
gressor of the rule;—that you have made me at length
as serious and severe as yourself:—but that the humours
you have stirred up might not work too potently within
me, I have waited four days to cool myself, before I
would set pen to paper to answer you, "*de mortuis nil
nisi bonum.*" I declare I have considered the wisdom
and foundation of it over and over again, as dispassion-
ately and charitably as a good Christian can, and, after
all, I can find nothing in it, or make more of it, than
a nonsensical lullaby of some nurse, put into Latin by
some pedant, to be chanted by some hypocrite to the
end of the world, for the consolation of departing
lechers.—'Tis, I own, Latin; and I think that is
all the weight it has—for, in plain English, 'tis a
loose and futile position below a dispute—"*you are
not to speak any thing of the dead, but what is good.*"
Why so?—Who says so?—neither reason nor scripture.
—Inspired authors have done otherwise—and reason
and common sense tell me, that if the characters of

past ages and men are to be drawn at all, they are to be
drawn like themselves; that is, with their excellencies,
and with their foibles—and it is as much a piece of
justice to the world, and to virtue too, to do the one,
as the other.—The ruling passion, *et les egaremens du
cœur*, are the very things which mark and distinguish a
man's character ;—in which I would as soon leave out
a man's head as his hobby-horse.—However, if like
the poor devil of a painter, we must conform to this pious
canon, *de mortuis*, &c., which I own has a spice of piety
in the *sound* of it, and be obliged to paint both our
angels and our devils out of the same pot—I then infer
that our Sydenhams, and Sangrados, our Lucretias, and
Messalinas, our Sommers, and our Bolingbrokes—are
alike entitled to statues, and all the historians or satirists
who have said otherwise since they departed this life,
from Sallust to S———e, are guilty of the crimes you
charge me with, " cowardice and injustice."

But why cowardice ? " because 'tis not courage to
attack a dead man who can't defend himself."—But
why do you doctors of the faculty attack such a one
with your incision knife ? Oh! for the good of the
living.—'Tis my plea.—But I have something more
to say in my behalf—and it is this—I am not guilty
of the charge—tho' defensible. I have not cut up
Doctor Kunastrokius at all—I have just scratch'd him
—and that scarce skin deep.—I do him first all honour
—speak of Kunastrokius as a great man—(be he whom
he will) and then most distantly hint at a drole foible
in his character—and that not first reported (to the few
who can even understand the hint) by me—but known
before by every chamber-maid and footman within the
bills of mortality—but Kunastrokius, you say, was a
great man—'tis that very circumstance which makes the
pleasantry—for I could name at this instant a score of
honest gentlemen who might have done the very thing

which Kunastrokius did, and seen no joke in it at all—
as to the failing of Kunastrokius, which you say can
only be imputed to his friends as a misfortune—I see
nothing like a misfortune in it to any friend or relation
of Kunastrokius—that Kunastrokius upon occasions
should sit with *** **** and *******——I have put
these stars not *to hurt your worship's delicacy*—If
Kunastrokius after all is too sacred a character to be
even smiled at (which is all I have done), he has had
better luck than his betters : In the same page (without
imputation of cowardice) I have said as much of a man
of twice his wisdom—and that is Solomon, of whom
I have made the same remark, " That they were both
great men—and like all mortal men had each their
ruling passion."

——The consolation you give me, " That my book,
however, will be read enough to answer my design of
raising a tax upon the public "—is very unconsolatory—
to say nothing how very mortifying! by h——n! an
author is worse treated than a common ***** at this
rate—" *You will get a penny by your sins, and that's
enough.*"—Upon this chapter let me comment.—That
I proposed laying the world under contribution when I
set pen to paper,—is what I own, and I suppose I may
be allow'd to have that view in my head in common
with every other writer, to make my labour of advantage
to myself.

Do you not do the same? but I beg I may add,
that whatever views I had of that kind, I had other
views—the first of which was, the hopes of doing the
world good, by ridiculing what I thought deserving of
it—or of disservice to sound learning, &c.—how I
have succeeded, my book must shew—and this I leave
entirely to the world—but not to that little world
of your acquaintance, whose opinion and sentiments
you call the general opinion of the best judges *without*

exception, who **all** affirm (you say) that my book cannot **be put into the** hands of any woman of *character*. (I hope you **except** widows, doctor—for **they are** not *all* **so** squeamish, **but I** am told they are **all** really of my party, in return **for** some good offices done their interests in the 274th page of my first volume.)   But for **the chaste** married, and chaste unmarried part of **the sex**— they must not read my book!   Heaven **forbid** the stock of chastity should be lessened by the **Life and** Opinions of Tristram Shandy—yes, his Opinions—it would certainly debauch 'em!   God take them under **his** protection in this fiery trial, and send us plenty of **Duennas** to watch the workings of their humours, till **they have** safely got through the whole work.—If this **will not be** sufficient, **may we have** plenty of Sangrados **to** pour in plenty **of** cold water, till this terrible fermentation is over—as for the *nummum in loculo*, which you mention to **me a** second time, **I fear you** think me very poor, **or** in debt——I thank **God**, though I don't abound—that **I** have enough for a clean shirt every day —and a mutton chop—and my contentment, with this, has thus far (and I **hope ever** will) put **me** above stooping an inch **for** it, **even for** ——'s estate.—Curse on it, I like it not to that degree, nor envy (*you* **may be** *sure*) any man who kneels in the dirt for it—so **that** howsoever I may fall short of the ends proposed in **commencing** author——I **enter** this *protest*, first **that** **my end was** *honest*, and secondly, that I wrote not **to** **be** *fed*, **but to** be *famous*.   I am much obliged to **Mr** Garrick **for** his very favourable opinion—but why, dear Sir, had he done better in finding **fault** with it than in commending it? to humble **me!** an **author is** not so soon humbled as **you** imagine—no, **but to** make the book better by castrations—that is still *sub judice*, and I can assure you upon this chapter, that the very passages and descriptions you propose that I should sacrifice in my second edition, are what are best relished by men of wit, and some others whom I esteem as sound critics—so that, upon the whole, I am still kept up, if not above fear, at least above despair, and have seen enough to show me the folly of an attempt of castrating my book to the prudish humours of particulars. I believe the short cut would be to publish this letter at the beginning of the third volume, as an apology for the first and second. I was sorry to find a censure upon the insincerity of some of my friends—I have no reason myself to reproach any one man—my friends have continued in the same opinions of my books which they first gave me of them—many indeed have thought better of 'em, by considering them more, few worse.

> I am, Sir,
> Your humble Servant,
> LAURENCE STERNE.

Letter vij.

To David Garrick, Esq.

[About April, 1760.]
Thursday, 11 o'clock—Night.

DEAR SIR,

'Twas for all the world like a cut across my finger with a sharp pen-knife. I saw the blood—gave it a suck—wrapt it up—and thought no more about it.

But there is more goes to the healing of a wound than this comes to:—a wound (unless it is a wound not worth talking of, but by the bye, mine is) must give you some pain after.—Nature will take her own way with it—it must ferment—it must digest.

The story you told me of Tristram's pretended tutor,

this morning—My letter by right should have set out
with this sentence, and then the simile would not have
kept you a moment in suspense.

This vile story, I say—though I then saw both
how, and where it wounded—I felt little from it at
first—or, to speak more honestly (though it ruins my
simile), I felt a great deal of pain from it, but affected
an air usual on such accidents, of less feeling than I
had.

I have now got home to my lodgings, since the play
(you astonished me in it), and have been unwrapping
this self-same wound of mine, and shaking my head
over it this half-hour.

What the devil!—is there no one learned block-
head throughout the many schools of misapplied science
in the Christian World, to make a *tutor* of for my
Tristram?—*Ex quovis ligno non fit*—Are we so run out
of stock, that there is no one lumber-headed, muddle-
headed, mortar-headed, pudding-headed *chap* amongst
our doctors?—Is there no one single wight of much
reading and no learning, amongst the many children in
my *mother's* nursery, who bid high for this charge—
but I must disable my judgment by chusing a Warburton? Vengeance! have I so little concern for the
honour of my hero!—Am I a wretch so void of sense,
so bereft of feeling for the figure he is to make in story,
that I should chuse a præceptor to rob him of all the
immortality I intended him? O! dear Mr Garrick.

Malice is ingenious—unless where the excess of it
outwits itself—I have two comforts in this stroke of it;
—the first is, that this one is partly of this kind; and
secondly, that it is one of the number of those which
so unfairly brought poor Yorick to his grave.—The
report might draw blood of the author of Tristram
Shandy—but could not harm such a man as the author
of the Divine Legation—God bless him! though (by

Dear Garrick.

Upon reviewing my finances this morning) w. some unforeseen expences — I find I should before with 20 £ of life — than a prudent man ought — will you lend me twenty pounds by

L. Sterne

the bye, and according to the natural course of descents) the blessing should come from him to me.

Pray have you no interest, lateral or collateral, to get me introduced to his Lordship?

Why do ye ask?

My dear Sir, I have no claim to such an honour, but what arises from the honour and respect which, in the progress of my work, will be shewn the world I owe to so great a man.

Whilst I am talking of owing—I wish, my dear Sir, that any body would tell you, how much I am indebted to you. I am determined never to do it myself, or say more upon the subject than this, that I am yours,

L. STERNE.

Letter viij.

To S—— C——, Esq.

DEAR SIR, May, 1760.

I RETURN you ten thousand thanks for the favour of your letter—and the account you give me of my wife and girl.—I saw Mr Ch——y to-night at Ranelagh, who tells me you have inoculated my friend Bobby.— I heartily wish him well through, and hope in God all goes right.

On Monday we set out with a grand retinue of Lord Rockingham's * (in whose suite I move) for Windsor—they have contracted for fourteen hundred pounds for the dinner, to some general undertaker, of which the K. has bargained to pay one third. Lord

---

* Prince Ferdinand, the Marquis of Rockingham, and Earl Temple, were installed Knights of the Garter, on Tuesday, May 6th, 1760, at Windsor.

George Sackville **was last** Saturday at the opera, some **say** with **great effrontery,—others**, with great dejection.

I have little news to add.—There is a shilling pamphlet * **wrote** against Tristram.—I wish they **would** write a hundred such.

Mrs Sterne says her purse is light; **will you, dear** Sir, be so good as to pay her **ten** guineas, and I will reckon with you, when I have the pleasure of **meeting** you.—My best compliments to Mrs C. and all friends. —Believe me, dear Sir, your obliged and faithful

LAU. STERNE.

Letter ix.

To the same.

May, 1760.

DEAR SIR,

I THIS **moment** received the favour **of your** kind letter. —The **letter** in **the** Ladies Magazine,† about me, was wrote by the noted Dr Hill, who wrote the Inspector, and undertakes **that** magazine—the people of York are very uncharitable to suppose any man **so** gross a beast as to pen such a character of himself.—In this great town no soul ever suspected it, for a thousand reasons—could they suppose I should be such a fool as to fall foul upon Dr Warburton, my best friend, **by** representing him **so weak** a man—or by telling **such** a lie of him—as **his** giving me a purse, to buy off his tutorship for Tristram!—or I should be fool enough **to** own I had taken his **purse** for that **purpose!**

You must know **there is** a quarrel between Dr Hill and Dr M———y, who **was** the physician meant at Mr Charles Stanhope's, and Dr Hill has changed the place

---

* "The Clockmaker's Outcry **against the** Author of Tristram Shandy." 8vo.

† The Royal Female Magazine, for April, 1760.

on purpose to give M——y a lick.—Now that conversation (though perhaps true), yet happened at another place,* and with another physician; which I have contradicted in this city, for the honour of my friend M——y, all which shews the absurdity of York credulity and nonsense. Besides, the account is full of falsehoods—first, with regard to the place of my

* As the truth of this anecdote is not denied, it may gratify curiosity to communicate it in Dr Hill's own words. "At the last dinner that the late lost amiable Charles Stanhope gave to genius, Yorick was present. The good old man was vexed to see a pedantic medicine-monger take the lead, and prevent that pleasantry which good wit and good wine might have occasioned, by a discourse in the unintelligible language of his profession, concerning the difference between the phrenitis and the paraphrenitis, and the concomitant categories of the mediastinum and pleura.

"Good-humoured Yorick saw the sense of the master of the feast, and fell into the cant and jargon of physic, as if he had been one of Radcliffe's travellers. 'The vulgar practice,' says he, 'savours too much of mechanical principles; the venerable ancients were all empirics, and the profession will never regain its ancient credit, till practice falls into the old track again. I am myself an instance; I caught cold by leaning on a damp cushion, and, after sneezing and sniveling a fortnight, it fell upon my breast: They blooded me, blistered me, and gave me robs and bobs, and lohocks and eclegmata; but I grew worse; for I was treated according to the exact rules of the College. In short, from an inflammation it came to an ADHESION, and all was over with me. They advised me to Bristol, that I might not do them the scandal of dying under their hands; and the Bristol people, for the same reason, consigned me over to Lisbon. But what do I? why I considered an adhesion is, in plain English, only a sticking of two things together, and that force enough would pull them asunder. I bought a good ash pole, and began leaping over all the walls and ditches in the country. From the height of the pole, I used to come souse down upon my feet, like an ass when he tramples upon a bull-dog: but it did not do. At last—when I had raised myself perpendicularly over a wall, I used to fall exactly across the ridge of it, upon the side opposite to the adhesion. This tore it off at once, and I am as you see. Come fill a glass to the memory of the empiric medicine.' If he had been asked elsewhere about this disorder (for he really had a consumptive disorder), he would have answered, that he was cured by Huxham's decoction of the bark, and elixir of vitriol."

birth, which was at Clonmel, in Ireland—the story of
a hundred pounds to Mrs W———,* not true, or of a
pension promised; the merit of which I disclaimed—
and indeed there are so many other things so untrue,
and unlikely to come from me, that the worst enemy I
have here never had a suspicion—and, to end all, Dr
Hill owns the paper.

I shall be down before May is out—I preach
before the Judges on Sunday—my Sermons come out
on Thursday after—and I purpose, the Monday,
at furthest, after that, to set out for York—I have
bought a pair of horses for that purpose—my best
respects to your Lady———

> I am, dear Sir,
> Your most obliged and faithful
> L. STERNE.

P.S.—I beg pardon for this hasty scrawl, having just
come from a concert where the D. of York performed.
—I have received great notice from him, and last week
had the honour of supping with him.

———

Letter x.

To Dr *Warburton, Bishop of Gloucester.*

MY LORD,   York, June 9, 1760.

Not knowing where to send two sets of my Sermons,
I could think of no better expedient, than to order
them into Mr Berrenger's hands, who has promised me
that he will wait upon your Lordship with them, the

* The widow of Mr Sterne's predecessor in the living of
Coxwould.

first moment he hears you are in town. The truest and humblest thanks I return to your Lordship, for the generosity of your protection, and advice to me, by making a good use of the one, I will hope to deserve the other; I wish your Lordship all the health and happiness in this world, for I am

Your Lordship's
Most obliged and
Most grateful Servant,
L. Sterne.

P.S.—I am just sitting down to go on with Tristram, &c.—The scribblers use me ill, but they have used my betters much worse, for which may God forgive them.

Letter xi.

To the Rev. Mr Sterne.

Prior-Park, June 15, 1760.

Reverend Sir,

I have your favour of the 9th instant, and am glad to understand, you are got safe home, and employed again in your proper studies and amusements. You have it in your power to make that, which is an amusement to yourself and others, useful to both: at least, you should above all things, beware of its becoming hurtful to either, by any violations of decency and good manners; but I have already taken such repeated liberties of advising you on that head, that to say more would be needless, or perhaps unacceptable.

Whoever is, in any way, well received by the public, is sure to be annoyed by that pest of the public, *profligate scribblers.* This is the common lot of successful adventurers;—but such have often a worse evil to struggle with, I mean the over-officiousness of their indiscreet friends. There are two Odes,* as they are called, printed by Dodsley. Whoever was the author, he appears to be a monster of impiety and lewdness—yet, such is the malignity of the scribblers, some have given them to your friend Hall;—and others, which is still more impossible, to yourself; though the first Ode has the insolence to place you both in a mean and a ridiculous light. But this might arise from a tale equally groundless and malignant, that you had shewn them to your acquaintances in MS. before they were given to the public. Nor was their being printed by Dodsley the likeliest means of discrediting the calumny.

About this time, another, under the mask of friendship, pretended to draw your character, which was since published in a *Female Magazine* (for dulness, who often has as great a hand as the devil, in deforming God's works of the creation, has *made them*, it seems, *male* and *female*), and from thence it was transferred into a *Chronicle*.† Pray have you read it, or do you know its author?

But of all these things, I dare say Mr Garrick, whose prudence is equal to his honesty or his talents, has remonstrated to you with the freedom of a friend. He knows the inconstancy of what is called the Public, towards all, even the best intentioned, of those who contribute to its pleasure or amusement. He (as every man of honour and discretion would) has availed himself of the public favour, to regulate the taste, and, in his proper station, to reform the manners of the

---

* Intitled, "Two Lyric Epistles: One to my Cousin Shandy, on his coming to Town; and the other to the Grown Gentlewomen, the Misses of ****." 4to.

† The London Chronicle, May 6, 1760.

fashionable world ;—while, by a well-judged œconomy, he has provided against the temptations of a mean and servile dependency on the follies and vices of the great.

In a word, be assured, there is no one more sincerely wishes your welfare and happiness, than,

Reverend Sir,

W. G.

Letter rij.

To my witty widow, Mrs F——.

Coxwould, Aug. 3, 1760.

MADAM,

WHEN a man's brains are as dry as a squeez'd Orange, —and he feels he has no more conceit in him than a Mallet, 'tis in vain to think of sitting down, and writing a letter to a lady of your wit, unless in the honest John-Trot-Style of, *yours of the 15th instant came safe to hand*, &c., which, by the bye, looks like a letter of business ; and you know very well, from the first letter I had the honour to write to you, I am a man of no business at all.   This vile plight I found my genius in was the reason I have told Mr ——, I would not write to you till the next post—hoping by that time to get some small recruit, at least of vivacity, if not wit, to set out with ;—but upon second thoughts, thinking a bad letter in season—to be better than a good one out of it—this scrawl is the consequence, which, if you will burn the moment you get it—I promise to send you a fine set essay in the style of your female episto-lizers, cut and trim'd at all points.—GOD defend me from such, who never yet knew what it was to say or write one premeditated word in my whole life—for this reason I send you this with pleasure, because wrote with the careless irregularity of an easy heart.——

Who told you, Garrick wrote the medley for Beard?
—'Twas wrote in his house, however, and before I
left town.——I deny it—I was not lost two days
before I left town.—I was lost all the time I was there,
and never found till I got to this Shandy-castle of
mine.—Next winter I intend to sojourn amongst you
with more decorum, and will neither be lost or found
any where.

Now I wish to GOD, I was at your elbow—I have
just finished one volume of Shandy, and I want to read
it to some one who I know can taste and relish humour—
this by the way, is a little impudent in me—for I take
the thing for granted, which their high mightinesses
the world have yet to determine—but I mean no such
thing—I could wish only to have your opinion—shall
I, in truth, give you mine?—I dare not—but I will;
provided you keep it to yourself—know then, that
I think there is more laughable humour,—with an
equal degree of Cervantic satire—if not more than in
the last—but we are bad judges of the merit of our
children.

I return you a thousand thanks for your friendly
congratulations upon my habitation—and I will take
care, you shall never wish me but well, for I am,
Madam,

With great esteem and truth,

Your most obliged,

L. STERNE.

P.S.—I have wrote this so vilely and so precipitately,
I fear you must carry it to a decypherer——I beg
you'll do me the honour to write—otherwise you draw
me in, instead of Mr —— drawing *you* into a scrape—
for I should sorrow to have a *taste* of so agreeable a
correspondent—and *no more.*

Adieu.

Letter xiii.

To S—— C——, Esq.

London, Christmas Day, 1760.

My dear Friend,

I have been in such a continual hurry since the moment I arrived here—what with my books, and what with visitors and visitings, that it was not in my power sooner to sit down and acknowledge the favour of your obliging letter; and to thank you for the most friendly motives which led you to write it: I am not much in pain upon what gives my kind friends at Stillington so much on the chapter of *Noses*—because, as the principal satire throughout that part is levelled at those learned blockheads, who, in all ages, have wasted their time and much learning upon points as foolish—it shifts off the idea of what you fear, to another point—and 'tis thought here very good—'twill pass muster—I mean not with all—no—no! I shall be attacked and pelted, either from cellars or garrets, write what I will—and besides, must expect to have a party against me of many hundreds—who either do not—or will not laugh.—— 'Tis enough if I divide the world;—at least I will rest contented with it.—I wish you was here to see what changes of looks and political reasoning have taken place in every company and coffee-house since last year; we shall be soon Prussians and Anti-Prussians, B——s and Anti-B——s, and those distinctions will just do as well as Whig and Tory—and for ought I know serve the same ends.——The King seems resolved to bring all things back to their original principles, and to stop the torrent of corruption and laziness. —He rises every morning at six to do business—rides out at eight to a minute, returns at nine to give himself up to his people.—By persisting, 'tis thought he will oblige his Ministers and dependants to dispatch affairs with him many hours sooner than of late—and 'tis much to be question'd whether they will not be enabled to wait upon him sooner by being freed from long levees of their own, and applications; which will in all likelihood be transferr'd from them directly to himself —the present system being to remove that phalanx of great people, which stood betwixt the throne and the subjects, and suffer them to have immediate access without the intervention of a cabal — (this is the language of others): however, the King gives every thing himself, knows every thing, and weighs every thing maturely, and then is inflexible—this puts old stagers off their game—how it will end we are all in the dark.

'Tis feared the war is quite over in Germany; never was known such havoc amongst troops—I was told yesterday by a Colonel from Germany, that out of two battalions of nine hundred men, to which he belonged, but seventy-one are left!—Prince Ferdinand has sent word, 'tis said, that he must have forty thousand men directly to take the field—and with provisions for them too, for he can but subsist them for a fortnight—I hope this will find you all got to York—I beg my compliments to the amiable Mrs Croft, &c. &c.

Tho' I purposed going first to Golden-Square, yet fate has thus long disposed of me—so I have never been able to set a foot towards that quarter.

I am, dear Sir,
Yours affectionately,
L. STERNE.

———

Letter ɹiv.

To the same.

[About Jan. 1761.]

MY DEAR SIR,

I HAVE just time to acknowledge the favour of yours, but not to get the two prints you mention—which shall be sent you by next post—I have bought them, and lent them to Miss Gilbert, but will assuredly send for them and enclose them to you:—I will take care to get your pictures well copied, and at a moderate price. And if I can be of further use, I beseech you to employ me; and from time to time will send you an account of whatever may be worth transmitting.—The stream now sets in strong against the German war. Loud complaints of —— —— —— making a trade of the war, &c. &c., much expected from Ld. Granby's evidence to these matters, who is expected every hour: —the King wins every day upon the people, shews himself much at the play (but at no opera), rides out with his brothers every morning, half an hour after seven, till nine—returns with them—spends an hour with them at breakfast and chat—and then sits down to business. I never dined at home once since I arrived—am fourteen dinners deep engaged just now, and fear matters will be worse with me in that point than better.—— As to the main points in view, at which you hint—all I can say is, that I see my way, and unless Old Nick throws the dice—shall, in due time, come off winner. ——Tristram will be out the twentieth—there is a great rout made about him before he enters the stage— whether this will be of use or no, I can't say—some wits of the first magnitude here, both as to wit and station, engage me success—time will shew—

Adieu.

Letter ꝗb.

To the same.

Dear Sir,   [March 1761.]

Since I had the favour of your obliging letter, nothing
has happened, or been said one day, which has not been
contradicted the next; so having little certain to
write, I have forebore writing at all, in hopes every day
of something worth filling up a letter. We had the
greatest expectations yesterday that ever were raised of
a pitched battle in the House of Commons, wherein
Mr Pitt was to have entered and thrown down the
gauntlet, in defence of the German war.—There never
was so full a house—the gallery full to the top—I was
there all the day—when lo! a political fit of the gout
seized the great combatant—he entered not the lists—
Beckford got up, and begged the house, as he saw not
his right honourable friend there, to put off the debate
—it could not be done; so Beckford rose up, and made
a most long, passionate, incoherent speech, in defence
of the Germanic war—but very severe upon the un-
frugal manner it was carried on—in which he addressed
himself principally to the Chancellor of the Exchequer,
and laid him on terribly.—It seems the chancery of
Hanover had laid out 350,000 pounds, on account,
and brought in our treasury debtor—and the grand
debate was, for an honest examination of the particulars
of this extravagant account, and for vouchers to authenti-
cate it.—Legge answered Beckford very rationally, and
coolly.—Lord N. spoke long—Sir F. Dashwood main-
tained the German war was most pernicious — Mr
C——, of Surry, spoke well against the account,
with some others—L. Barrington at last got up, and
spoke half an hour with great plainness, and temper—

explained a great many hidden springs relating to these accounts, in favour of the late King, and told two or three conversations which had passed between the King and himself, relative to these expences—which cast great honour upon the King's character. This was with regard to the money the King had secretly furnished out of his pocket to lessen the account of the Hanover-score brought us to discharge.

Beckford and Barrington abused all who sought for peace, and joined in the cry for it; and Beckford added, that the reasons of wishing a peace now, were the same as the peace of Utrecht—that the people behind the curtain could not both maintain the war and their places too, so were for making another sacrifice of the nation, to their own interests—After all—the cry for a peace is so general, that it will certainly end in one. Now for myself.——

One half of the town abuse my book as bitterly, as the other half cry it up to the skies—the best is, they abuse and buy it, and at such a rate, that we are going on with a second edition, as fast as possible.

I am going down for a day or two with Mr Spencer, to Wimbleton; on Wednesday there is to be a grand assembly at Lady N——. I have enquired every where about Stephen's affair, and can hear nothing— My friend, Mr Charles Townshend, will be now secretary of war *—he bid me wish him joy of it, though not in possession—I will ask him—and depend, my most worthy friend, that you shall not be ignorant of what I learn from him—Believe me ever, ever,

Yours,

L. S.

* He was appointed Secretary at war the 24th of March 1761.

Letter xvi.

To the same.

My dear Sir, [April **1761**.]

A strain which I got in my wrist by a terrible fall, prevented my acknowledging the favour of your obliging letter. I went yesterday morning to breakfast with Mr V——, who is a kind of right hand man to the secretary, on purpose to enquire about the propriety, **or** feasibility, of doing what you wish me—and he **has told** me an anecdote which, had you been here, would, I think, have made **it wiser to** have deferred speaking about the affair a month **hence than** now: it is this— You must know that the numbers of officers who have **left** their regiments **in** Germany, for **the** pleasures of **the town, have** been long a topic **for** merriment; as you see **them in** St James's Coffee-house, and the park, every hour, enquiring, open **mouth, how** things go on in Germany, and what news;—when they should have been there to have furnished news themselves—but the worst part has been, that many of them have left their brother officers on their duty, and in all the fatigues of it, and have come **with** no end but to make friends, **to** be put unfairly over the *heads of those* who were **left** risking *their lives.*—In this attempt there have been some but too successful, which has justly raised ill-**blood and** complaints from the officers who staid behind — the upshot has been, that **they** have every soul been ordered off, and woe be to **him** ('tis said) who shall be found listening! Now just **to** mention our friend's **case** whilst this **cry** is on foot, I think would be doing more hurt than good; but if you think otherwise, I will go with all my heart, and mention it to Mr Townshend, for **to** do more I am too inconsiderable a person to pretend to.—You made me and my friends here very merry with the accounts current at York, of my being forbid the court—but they do not consider what a considerable person they make of me, when they suppose either my going, or my not going there, is a point that ever enters the King's head—and for those about him, I have the honour either to stand so personally well known to them, or to be so well represented by those of the first rank, as to fear no accident of that kind.

I thank GOD (B——'s excepted) I have never yet made a friend or connection I have forfeited, or done ought to forfeit—but, on the contrary, my true character is better understood, and where I had one friend last year, who did me honour, I have three now. —If my enemies knew, that by this rage of abuse, and ill-will, they were effectually serving the interests both of myself, and works, they would be more quiet—but it has been the fate of my betters, who have found, that the way to fame, is like the way to heaven— through much tribulation—and till I shall have the honour to be as much mal-treated as Rabelais and Swift were, I must continue humble;—for I have not filled up the measure of half their *persecutions*.

The court is turning topsy-turvy. Lord Bute, le premier *—Lord Talbot, to be groom of the chambers † in room of the D. of R——d—Lord Hallifax to Ireland ‡—Sir F. Dashwood in Talbot's place—Pitt seems unmoved—a peace inevitable— Stocks rise—the peers this moment kissing hands, &c. &c. (this week may be christened the kiss-hands week)

---

* Lord Bute was appointed Secretary of State on the 25th of March 1761.

† Lord Talbot was appointed Steward of the household on the same day.

‡ Lord Hallifax was appointed Lord Lieutenant of Ireland on the 20th of March 1761.

for a hundred changes will happen in consequence of these. Pray present my compliments to Mrs C. and all friends, and believe me, with the greatest fidelity,

Your ever obliged
L. STERNE.

P.S.—Is it not strange that Lord Talbot should have power to remove the Duke of R——d?

Pray when you have read this, send the news to Mrs Sterne.

Letter xvii.

To J—— H—— S——, Esq.

DEAR H——, Coxwould, July 28, 1761.

I SYMPATHISED for, or with you, on the detail you give me of your late agitations—and would willingly have taken my horse, and trotted to the oracle to have enquired into the etymology of all your sufferings, had I not been assured, that all that evacuation of bilious matter, with all that abdominal motion attending it (both which are equal to a month's purgation and exercise) will have left you better than it found you—Need one go to D——, to be told that all kind of mild (mark, I am going to talk more foolishly than your apothecary), opening, saponacious, dirty-shirt, sud-washing liquors are proper for you, and consequently all styptical potations, death and destruction—if you had not shut up your gall-ducts by these, the glauber-salts could not have hurt—as it was, 'twas like a match to the gunpowder, by raising a fresh combustion, as all physic does at first, so that you have been let off—nitre, brimstone, and charcoal (which is blackness itself), all at one blast—'twas well the piece did not burst, for I think it underwent great violence, and, as it is proof, will, I hope, do much service in this militating world—Panty* is mistaken, I quarrel with no one.—There was that coxcomb of —— in the house, who lost temper with me for no reason upon earth but that I could not fall down and worship a brazen image of learning and eloquence, which he set up, to the persecution of all true believers—I sat down upon *his altar*, and whistled in the time of his divine service—and broke down his carved work, and kicked his incense pot to the D——, so he retreated, *sed non sine felle in corde suo.*—I have wrote a clerum, whether I shall take my doctor's degrees or no—I am much in doubt, but I trow not.—I go on with Tristram—I have bought seven hundred books at a purchase dog cheap—and many good—and I have been a week getting them set up in my best room here—why do not you transport yours to town, but I talk like a fool.—This will just catch you at your spaw—I wish you *incolumem apud Londinum*—do you go there for good and all—or ill?—I am, dear cousin,

Yours affectionately,
L. STERNE.

Letter xviii.

To the same.

Coxwould [about August], 1761.

DEAR H——,

I REJOICE you are in London—rest you there in peace : —here 'tis the devil.—You was a good prophet.—I wish myself back again, as you told me I should—but

* The Reverend Mr R—— L——.

not because a thin, death-doing, pestiferous, north-east wind blows in a line directly from Crazy-castle turret full upon me in this cuckoldy retreat (for I value the north-east wind and all its powers not a straw),—but the transition from rapid motion to absolute rest was too violent.—I should have walked about the streets of York ten days, as a proper medium to have passed through, before I entered upon my rest.—I staid but a moment, and I have been here but a few, to satisfy me I have not managed my miseries like a wise man—and if God, for my consolation under them, had not poured forth the spirit of Shandeism into me, which will not suffer me to think two moments upon any grave subject, I would else, just now lie down and die—die———and yet, in half an hour's time, I'll lay a guinea, I shall be as merry as a monkey—and as mischievous too, and forget it all—so that this is but a copy of the present train running cross my brain.—And so you think this cursed stupid—but that, my dear H., depends much upon the quotâ horâ of your shabby clock, if the pointer of it is in any quarter between ten in the morning or four in the afternoon—I give it up—or if the day is obscured by dark engendering clouds of either wet or dry weather, I am still lost—but who knows but it may be five—and the day as fine a day as ever shone upon the earth since the destruction of Sodom,—and peradventure your honour may have got a good hearty dinner to-day, and eat and drank your intellectuals into a placidulish and a blandulish amalgama—to bear nonsense, so much for that.

'Tis as cold and churlish just now, as (if God had not pleased it to be so) it ought to have been in bleak December, and therefore I am glad you are where you are, and where (I repeat it again) I wish I was also—Curse of poverty, and absence from those we love!—they are two great evils which embitter all things—and yet with the first I am not haunted much.—As to matrimony, I should be a beast to rail at it, for my wife is easy—but the world is not—and had I staid from her a second longer, it would have been a burning shame —else she declares her self happier without me—but not in anger is this declaration made—but in pure sober good-sense, built on sound experience—-she hopes you will be able to strike a bargain for me before this time twelvemonth, to lead a bear round Europe: and from this hope from you, I verily believe it is, that you are so high in her favour at present—She swears you are a fellow of wit, though humorous; a funny, jolly soul, though somewhat splenetic; and (bating the love of women) as honest as *gold*—how do you like the simile? —Oh, Lord! now are you going to Ranelagh to-night, and I am sitting, sorrowful as the prophet was, when the voice cried out to him and said, "What dost thou here, Elijah?"—'Tis well the spirit does not make the same at Coxwould—for unless for the few sheep left me to take care of, in this wilderness, I might as well, nay better, be at Mecca—When we find we can, by a shifting of places, run away from ourselves, what think you of a jaunt there, before we finally pay a visit to the *vale of Jehosaphat?*—As ill a fame as we have, I trust I shall one day or other see you face to face— so tell the two colonels, if they love good company, to live righteously and soberly, as *you do*, and then they will have no doubts or dangers within or without them —present my best and warmest wishes to them, and advise the eldest to prop up his spirits, and get a rich dowager before the conclusion of the peace—why will not the advice suit both, *par nobile fratrum?*

To-morrow morning (if Heaven permit) I begin the fifth volume* of Shandy—I care not a curse for the critics—I'll load my vehicle with what goods *he*

* Alluding to the first edition.

sends me, and they may take 'em off my hands, or let them alone—I am very valorous—and 'tis in proportion as we retire from the world, and see it in its true dimensions, that we despise it—no bad rant!—God above bless you! You know I am

Your affectionate Cousin,

LAURENCE STERNE.

What few remain of the Demoniacs, greet—and write me a letter, if you are able, as foolish as this.

Letter rir.

To Lady ——.

Coxwould, **Sept. 21, 1761.**

I RETURN to my new habitation, fully determined to write as hard as can be, and thank you most cordially, my dear lady, for your letter of congratulation upon my Lord Fauconberg's having presented me with the curacy of this place—though your congratulation comes somewhat of the latest, as I have been possessed of it some time.—I hope I have been of some service to his Lordship, and he has sufficiently requited me.— 'Tis seventy guineas a year in my pocket, though worth a hundred—but it obliges me to have a curate to officiate at Sutton and Stillington.—'Tis within a mile of his Lordship's seat and park. 'Tis a very agreeable ride out in the chaise I purchased for my wife.—Lyd has a poney which she delights in.— Whilst they take these diversions, I am scribbling away at my Tristram. These two volumes are, I think, the best.—I shall write as long as I live, 'tis, in fact, my hobby-horse: and so much am I delighted with my uncle Toby's imaginary character, that I am become an enthusiast.—My Lydia helps to copy for me—and my wife knits, and listens as I read her chapters.—The coronation of his Majesty (whom GOD preserve!) has cost me the value of an ox, which is to be roasted whole in the middle of the town, and my parishioners will, I suppose, be very merry upon the occasion.—You will then be in town—and feast your eyes with a sight, which 'tis to be hoped will not be in either of our powers to see again—for in point of age we have about twenty years the start of his Majesty.— And now, my dear friend, I must finish this—and with every wish for your happiness conclude myself your most sincere well-wisher and friend,

L. STERNE.

Letter II.

To David Garrick, Esq.

Paris, Jan. 31, 1762.

MY DEAR FRIEND,

THINK not, because I have been a fortnight in this metropolis without writing to you, that therefore I have not had you and Mrs Garrick a hundred times in my head and heart—heart! yes, yes, say you—but I must not waste paper in *badinage* this post, whatever I do the next. Well! here I am, my friend, as much improved in my health, for the time, as ever your friendship could wish, or at least your faith give credit to—by the bye I am somewhat worse in my intellectuals, for my head is turned round with what I see, and the unexpected honours I have met with here. Tristram was almost as much known here as in London, at least among your men of condition and

learning, and has got me introduced into so many circles
('tis *comme à Londres*). I have just now a fortnight's
dinners and suppers upon my hands—My application to the Count de Choiseul goes on swimmingly,
for not only Mr. Pelletiere (who, by the bye, sends
ten thousand civilities to you and Mrs Garrick) has
undertaken my affair, but the Count de Limbourgh—
the Baron d'Holbach, has offered any security for the
inoffensiveness of my behaviour in France—'tis more,
you rogue! than you will do—This Baron is one of
the most learned noblemen here, the great protector of
wits, and the Sçavans who are no wits—keeps open
house three days a week—his house is now, as yours
was to me, my own—he lives at great expence—'Twas
an odd incident when I was introduced to the Count
de Bissie, which I was at his desire—I found him
reading Tristram—this grandee does me great honours,
and gives me leave to go a private way through his
apartments into the palais royal, to view the Duke of
Orleans's collections, every day I have time—I have
been at the doctors of Sorbonne—I hope in a fortnight
to break through, or rather from, the delights of this
place, which, in the *sçavoir vivre*, exceeds all the
places, I believe, in this section of the globe——

I am going, when this letter is wrote, with Mr Fox
and Mr Maccartny to Versailles—the next morning I
wait upon Mons. Titon, in company with Mr Maccartny,
who is known to him, to deliver your commands.—I
have bought you the pamphlet upon theatrical, or rather
tragical, declamation—I have bought another in verse,
worth reading, and you will receive them, with what
I can pick up this week, by a servant of Mr Hodges,
whom he is sending back to England.

I was last night with Mr Fox to see Mademoiselle
Clairon, in *Iphigene*—she is extremely great—would to
God you had one or two like her—what a luxury, to

see you with one of such powers in the same interesting scene—but 'tis too much—Ah! Preville! thou art Mercury himself—By virtue of taking a couple of boxes, we have bespoke, this week, *The Frenchman in London*, in which Preville is to send us home to supper, *all happy*—I mean about fifteen or sixteen English of distinction, who are now here, and live well with each other.

I am under great obligations to Mr Pitt, who has behaved in every respect to me like a man of good breeding, and good nature—In a post or two, I will write again—Foley is an honest soul—I could write six volumes of what has passed comically in this great scene, since these last fourteen days—but more of this hereafter.—We are all going into mourning; nor you, nor Mrs Garrick, would know me, if you met me in my *remise*—bless you both! Service to Mrs Denis. Adieu, adieu!

L. S.

Letter xxi.

To Lady D——.

London,* Feb. 1, 1762.

Your Ladyship's kind enquiries after my health are indeed kind, and of a piece with the rest of your character. Indeed I am very ill, having broke a vessel in my lungs—hard writing in the summer, together with preaching, which I have not strength for, is ever fatal to me—but I cannot avoid the latter yet, and the former is too pleasurable to be given up—I believe I shall try if the south of France will not be of service to me—his G. of Y. has most humanely given

---

* This Letter, though dated from *London*, was evidently written at *Paris*.

me the permission for a year or two—I shall set off with great hopes of its efficacy, and shall write to my wife and daughter to come and join me at Paris, else my stay could not be so long—" Le Fever's story has beguiled your Ladyship of your tears," and the thought of the accusing spirit flying up to heaven's chancery with the oath, you are kind enough to say is sublime—my friend, Mr Garrick, thinks so too, and I am most vain of his approbation—your Ladyship's opinion adds not a little to my vanity.

I wish I had time to take a little excursion to Bath, were it only to thank you for all the obliging things you say in your letter—but 'tis impossible—accept at least my warmest thanks—If I could tempt my friend Mr H. to come to France, I should be truly happy —If I can be of any service to you at Paris, command him who is, and ever will be,

Your Ladyship's faithful

L. STERNE.

Letter xxij.

To David Garrick, Esq.

DEAR GARRICK,   Paris, March 19, 1762.

THIS will be put into your hands by Dr Shippen, a physician, who has been here some time with Miss Poyntz, and is this moment setting off for your metropolis; so I snatch the opportunity of writing to you and my kind friend Mrs Garrick.—I see nothing like her here, and yet I have been introduced to one half of their best Goddesses, and in a month more shall be admitted to the shrines of the other half—but I neither worship—or fall (much) upon my knees before them;

but, on the contrary, have converted many unto Shandeism—for be it known, I Shandy it away fifty times
more than I was ever wont, talk more nonsense than
ever you heard me talk in your days—and to all sorts
of people. *Qui le diable est cet homme là*—said Choiseul,
t'other day—*ce Chevalier Shandy*—You'll think me as
vain as a devil, was I to tell you the rest of the dia-
logue—whether the bearer knows it or no, I know not
—'Twill serve up after supper, in Southampton-street,
amongst other small dishes, after the fatigues of Richard
the IIId—O God! they have nothing here, which gives
the nerves so smart a blow, as those great characters
in the hands of Garrick! but I forgot I am writing
to the man himself——The devil take (as he will)
these transports of enthusiasm! Apropos—the whole
City of Paris is *bewitch'd* with the comic opera, and if
it was not for the affair of the Jesuits, which takes up
one half of our talk, the comic opera would have it all
—It is a tragical nuisance in all companies as it is, and
was it not for some sudden starts and dashes—of
Shandeism, which now and then either break the thread,
or entangle it so, that the devil himself would be puzzled
in winding it off—I should die a martyr—this by the
way I never will——

I send you over some of these comic operas by the
bearer, with the *Sallon*, a satire—The French comedy,
I seldom visit it—they act scarce any thing but tragedies
—and the Clairon is great, and Mad^{lle} Dumesnil, in
some places, still greater than her—yet I cannot bear
preaching—I fancy I got a surfeit of it in my younger
days.—There is a tragedy to be damn'd to-night—
peace be with it, and the gentle brain which made it!
I have ten thousand things to tell you I cannot write—
I do a thousand things which cut no figure, *but in the
doing*—and as in London, I have the honour of having
done and said a thousand things I never did or dream'd

of—and yet I dream abundantly—If the devil stood behind me in the shape of a courier, I could not write faster than I do, having five letters more to dispatch by the same Gentleman ; he is going into another section of the globe, and when he has seen you, he will depart in peace.

The Duke of Orleans has suffered my portrait to be added to the number of some odd men in his collection ; and a gentleman who lives with him has taken it most expressively, at full length—I purpose to obtain an etching of it, and to send it you—your prayer for me of *rosy health*, is heard—If I stay here for three or four months, I shall return more than reinstated. My love to Mrs Garrick.

I am, my dear Garrick,

Your most humble Servant,

L. STERNE.

Letter xxiij.

To the same.

My DEAR GARRICK,   Paris, April 10, 1762.

I SNATCH the occasion of Mr Wilcox (the late Bishop of Rochester's son) leaving this place for England, to write to you, and I enclose it to Hall, who will put it into your hand, possibly behind the scenes. I hear no news of you, or your *empire*, I would have said *kingdom* —but here every thing is hyperbolized—and if a woman is but simply pleased—'tis *Je suis charmé*—and if she is charmed, 'tis nothing less than that she is *ravi*-sh'd —and when ravi-sh'd (which may happen) there is nothing left for her but to fly to the other world for a metaphor, and swear, qu'elle étoit tout *extasiée*—which mode of speaking is, by the bye, here creeping into use,

63

and there is scarce a woman who understands the *bon ton* but is seven times in a day in downright extasy— that is, the devil's in her—by a small mistake of one world for the other——Now, where am I got?

I have been these two days reading a tragedy, given me by a lady of talents to read, and conjecture if it would do for you—'Tis from the plan of Diderot, and possibly half a translation of it.—The Natural Son, or the Triumph of Virtue, in five acts—It has too much sentiment in it (at least for me), the speeches too long, and savour too much of *preaching*—this may be a second reason, it is not to my taste—'Tis all love, love, love, throughout, without much separation in the character; so I fear it would not do for your stage, and perhaps for the very reasons which recommend it to a French one.—After a vile suspension of three weeks—we are beginning with our comedies and operas again—yours I hear never flourished more—here the comic actors were never so low—the tragedians hold up their heads —in all senses. I have known *one little man* support the theatrical world, like a David Atlas, upon his shoulders, but Preville can't do half as much here, though Mad^{lle} Clairon stands by him, and sets her back to his—she is very great, however, and highly improved since you saw her—she also supports her dignity at table, and has her public day every Thursday, when she *gives to eat* (as they say here) to all that are hungry and dry.

You are much talked of here, and much expected as soon as the peace will let you—these two last days you have happened to engross the whole conversation at two great houses where I was at dinner—'Tis the greatest problem in nature, in this meridian, that one and the same man should possess such tragic and comic powers, and in such an equilibrio, as to divide the world for which of the two Nature intended him.

Crebillion has made a convention with me, which, if he is not too lazy, will be no bad *persiflage*—as soon as I get to Toulouse he has agreed to write me an expostulatory letter upon the indecorums of T. Shandy —which is to be answered by recrimination upon the liberties in his own works—these are to be printed together—Crebillion against Sterne—Sterne against Crebillion—the copy to be sold, and the money equally divided—This is good Swiss-policy.

I am recovered greatly, and if I could spend one whole winter at Toulouse, I should be fortified, in my inner man, beyond all danger of relapsing. — A sad asthma my daughter has been martyr'd with these three winters, but mostly this last, makes it, I fear, necessary she should try the last remedy of a warmer and softer air, so I am going this week to Versailles, to wait upon Count Choiseul to solicit passports for them—If this system takes place, they join me here— and after a month's stay we all decamp for the south of France—if not, I shall see you in June next. Mr Fox, and Mr Maccartny, having left Paris, I live altogether in French families—I laugh till I cry, and in the same tender moments *cry till I laugh*. I Shandy it more than ever, and verily do believe, that by mere Shandeism, sublimated by a laughter-loving people, I fence as much against infirmities, as I do by the benefit of air and climate. Adieu, dear Garrick! present ten thousand of my best respects and wishes to and for my friend Mrs Garrick — had she been last night upon the Tuilleries, she would have anni- hilated a thousand French goddesses, *in one single turn.*

I am, most truly,

My dear friend,

L. STERNE.

Letter xxii.

To Mrs Sterne, York.

Paris, May 16th, 1762.

MY DEAR,

IT is a thousand to one that this reaches you before you have set out—However I take the chance—you will receive one wrote last night, the moment you get to Mr E. and to wish you joy of your arrival in town—to that letter which you will find in town, I have nothing to add that I can think on—for I have almost drain'd my brains dry upon the subject. —For GOD's sake rise early and gallop away in the cool—and always see that you have not forgot your baggage in changing post-chaises —— You will find good tea upon the road from York to Dover—only bring a little to carry you from Calais to Paris—give the Custom-House Officers what I told you—at Calais give more, if you have much Scotch snuff —but as tobacco is good here, you had best bring a Scotch mill and make it yourself, that is, order your valet to manufacture it—'twill keep him out of mischief. — I would advise you to take three days in coming up, for fear of heating yourselves—See that they do not give you a bad vehicle, when a better is in the yard, but you will look sharp—drink small Rhenish to keep you cool (that is, if you like it). Live well, and deny yourselves nothing your hearts wish. So GOD in heaven prosper and go along with you—kiss my Lydia, and believe me both affectionately,

Yours,

L. STERNE.

———

I.

E

Letter xxv.

To the same.

My Dear,

THERE have no mails arrived here till this morning, for three posts, so I expected with great impatience a letter from you and Lydia—and lo! it is arrived. You are as busy as Throp's wife, and by the time you receive this, you will be busier still—I have exhausted all my ideas about your journey—and what is needful for you to do before and during it—so I write only to tell you I am well—Mr Colebrooks, the minister of Swisserland's secretary, I got this morning to write a letter for you to the governor of the Custom-House Office, at Calais—it shall be sent you next post.—You must be cautious about Scotch snuff—take half a pound in your pocket, and make Lyd do the same. 'Tis well I bought you a chaise—there is no getting one in Paris now, but at an enormous price—for they are all sent to the army, and such a one as yours we have not been able to match for forty guineas, for a friend of mine who is going from hence to Italy—the weather was never known to set in so hot, as it has done the latter end of this month, so he and his party are to get into his chaises by four in the morning, and travel till nine—and not stir out again till six ;—but I hope this severe heat will abate by the time you come here—however, I beg of you once more to take special care of heating your blood in travelling, and come *tout doucement*, when you find the heat too much —I shall look impatiently for intelligence from you, and hope to hear all goes well ; that you conquer all difficulties, that you have received your pass-port, my picture, &c. Write and tell me something of every thing. I long to see you both, you may be assured, my dear wife and child, after so long a separation—— and write me a line directly, that I may have all the notice you can give me, that I may have apartments ready and fit for you when you arrive.—For my own part I shall continue writing to you a fortnight longer —present my respects to all friends—you have bid Mr C. get my visitations at P. done for me, &c. &c. If any offers are made about the inclosure at Rascal, they must be enclosed to me—nothing that is fairly proposed shall stand still on my score. Do all for the best, as He who guides all things will I hope do for us—so heaven preserve you both—believe me

Your affectionate
L. Sterne.

Love to my Lydia — I have bought her a gold watch to present to her when she comes.

***

Letter xxvi.

To the same.

Paris, June 7, 1762.

My Dear,

I keep my promise and write to you again——I am sorry the bureau must be open'd for the deeds—but you will see it done—I imagine you are convinced of the necessity of bringing three hundred pounds in your pocket —if you consider, Lydia must have two slight negligees —you will want a new gown or two—as for painted linens, buy them in town, they will be more admired because English than French.—Mrs H. writes me word that I am mistaken about buying silk cheaper at Toulouse than Paris, that she advises you to buy what you want here—where they are very beautiful and

cheap, as well as blonds, gauzes, &c.—These I say
will all cost you sixty guineas—and you must have
them—for in this country nothing must be spared for
the back—and if you dine on an onion, and lie in a
garret seven stories high, you must not betray it in
your cloaths, according to which you are well or ill
look'd on.   When we are got to Toulouse, we must
begin to turn the penny, and we may (if you do not
game much) live very cheap—I think that expression
will divert you—and now GOD knows I have not a
wish but for your health, comfort, and safe arrival here
—write to me every other post, that I may know how
you go on—you will be in raptures with your chariot
—Mr R. a gentleman of fortune, who is going to Italy,
and has seen it, has offered me thirty guineas for my
bargain.—You will wonder all the way, how I am to
find room in it for a third—to ease you of this wonder,
'tis by what the coachmakers here call a cave, which
is a second bottom added to that you set your feet
upon, which lets the person (who sits over-against
you) down with his knees to your ancles, and by
which you have all more room—and what is more,
less heat,—because his head does not intercept the
fore-glass—little or nothing—Lyd and I will enjoy
this by turns; sometimes I shall take a bidet—(a little
post horse) and scamper before—at other times I shall
sit in fresco upon the arm-chair without doors, and
one way or other will do very well.—I am under infinite obligations to Mr Thornhill, for accommodating
me thus, and so genteelly, for 'tis like making a present
of it.—Mr T—— will send you an order to receive it
at Calais—and now, my dear girls, have I forgot any
thing?

Adieu! adieu!
Yours most affectionately,
L. STERNE.

A week or ten days will enable you to see every thing—and so long you must stay to rest your bones.

Letter ꭓꭓbij.

To the same.

MY DEAREST, Paris, June 14, 1762.

HAVING an opportunity of writing by a friend who is setting out this morning for London, I write again, in case the two last letters I have wrote this week to you should be detained by contrary winds at Calais—I have wrote to Mr E——, by the same hand, to thank him for his kindness to you in the handsomest manner I could—and have told him, his good heart, and his wife's, have made them overlook the trouble of having you at his house, but that if he takes you apartments near him, they will have occasion still enough left to shew their friendship to us—I have begged him to assist you, and stand by you as if he was in my place, with regard to the sale of the Shandys—and then the copyright—Mark to keep these things distinct in your head—But Becket I have ever found to be a man of probity, and I dare say you will have very little trouble in finishing matters with him—and I would rather wish you to treat with him than with another man—but whoever buys the fifth and sixth volumes of Shandy's, must have the nay-say of the seventh and eighth.*— I wish, when you come here, in case the weather is too hot to travel, you could think it pleasant to go to the Spa for four or six weeks, where we should live for half the money we should spend at Paris—after

* Alluding to the first edition.

that, we should take the sweetest season of the vintage to go to the south of France—but we will put our heads together, and you shall just do as you please in this, and in every thing which depends on me—for I am a being perfectly contented, when others are pleased —to bear and forbear will ever be my maxim—only I fear the heats through a journey of five hundred miles for you, and my Lydia, more than for myself.—Do not forget the watch-chains—bring a couple for a gentleman's watch likewise; we shall lie under great obligations to the Abbé M., and must make him such a small acknowledgment; according to my way of flourishing, 'twill be a present worth a kingdom to him —They have bad pins, and vile needles here—bring for yourself, and some for presents—as also a strong bottle-skrew, for whatever Scrub we may hire as butler, coachman, &c., to uncork us our Frontiniac—You will find a letter for you at the Lyon D'Argent—Send for your chaise into the court-yard, and see all is right— Buy a chain, at Calais, strong enough not to be cut off, and let your portmanteau be tied on the forepart of your chaise for fear of a dog's trick—so GOD bless you both, and remember me to my Lydia.

> I am yours affectionately,
> L. STERNE.

Letter rrbiij.

To the same.

Paris, June 17, 1762.

MY DEAREST,

PROBABLY you will receive another letter with this, by the same post—if so, read this the last—It will be the last you can possibly receive at York, for I hope it will catch you just as you are upon the wing—if that should happen, I suppose in course you have executed the contents of it, in all things which relate to pecuniary matters, and when these are settled to your mind, you will have got through your last difficulty—every thing else will be a step of pleasure, and by the time you have got half a dozen stages, you will set up your pipes and sing Te Deum together, as you whisk it along.—Desire Mr C—— to send me a proper letter of attorney by you, he will receive it back by return of post. You have done every thing well with regard to our Sutton and Stillington affairs, and left things in the best channel —if I was not sure you must have long since got my picture, garnets, &c., I would write and scold Mr T—— abominably—he put them in Becket's hands to be forwarded by the stage-coach to you, as soon as he got to town.—I long to hear from you, and that all my letters and things are come safe to you, and then you will say that I have not been a bad lad—for you will find I have been writing continually, as I wished you to do—Bring your silver coffee-pot, 'twill serve both to give water, lemonade, and or jead—to say nothing of coffee and chocolate, which, by the bye, is both cheap and good at Toulouse, like other things—I had like to have forgot a most necessary thing, there are no copper tea-kettles to be had in France, and we shall find such a thing the most comfortable utensil in the house—buy a good strong one, which will hold two quarts—a dish of tea will be of comfort to us in our journey south—— I have a bronze tea-pot, which we will carry also—as china cannot be brought over from England, we must make up a villanous party-coloured tea equipage, to regale ourselves, and our English friends, whilst we are at Toulouse—I hope you have got your bill from Becket.—There is a good-natured kind of a trader I have just heard of, at Mr Foley's, who they think will be coming off from England to France, with horses, the latter end of June. He happened to come over with a lady, who is sister to Mr Foley's partner, and I have got her to write a letter to him in London, this post, to beg he will seek you out at Mr E——'s, and, in case a cartel ship does not go off before he goes, to take you under his care. He was infinitely friendly, in the same office, last year, to the lady who now writes to him, and nursed her on ship-board, and defended her by land with great good-will. Do not say I forget you, or whatever can be conducive to your ease of mind, in this journey—I wish I was with you, to do these offices myself, and to strew roses on your way—but I shall have time and occasion to shew you I am not wanting—Now, my dears, once more pluck up your spirits—trust in GOD—in me—and in yourselves—with this, was you put to it, you would encounter all these difficulties ten times told—Write instantly, and tell me you triumph over all fears; tell me Lydia is better, and a helpmate to you—You say she grows like me—let her shew me she does so in her contempt of small dangers, and fighting against the apprehensions of them, which is better still. As I will not have F.'s share of the books, you will inform him so—Give my love to Mr Fothergill, and to those true friends which Envy has spared me—and for the rest, *laissez passer*—You will find I speak French tolerably—but I only wish to be understood.—You will soon speak better; a month's play with a French Demoiselle will make Lyd chatter like a magpye. Mrs —— understood not a word of it when she got here, and writes me word she begins to prate apace— you will do the same in a fortnight—Dear Bess, I have a thousand wishes, but have a hope for every one of them—you shall chant the same *jubilate*, my dears, so

God bless you. My duty to Lydia, which implies my love too. Adieu, believe me

Your affectionate

L. Sterne.

Memorandum : Bring watch - chains, tea - kettle, knives, cookery-book, &c.

You will smile at this last article—so adieu—At Dover, the Cross Keys ; at Calais, the Lyon D'Argent —the master, a Turk in grain.

Letter xxix.

To Lady D.

Paris, July 9, 1762.

I will not send your ladyship the trifles you bid me purchase without a line. I am very well pleased with Paris—indeed I meet with so many civilities amongst the people here, that I must sing their praises—the French have a great deal of urbanity in their composition, and to stay a little time amongst them will be agreeable.—I splutter French so as to be understood— but I have had a droll adventure here in which my Latin was of some service to me—I had hired a chaise and a horse to go about seven miles into the country, but, *Shandean-like*, did not take notice that the horse was almost dead when I took him—Before I got half-way, the poor animal dropped down dead—so I was forced to appear before the Police, and began to tell my story in French, which was, that the poor beast had to do with a worse beast than himself, namely *his master*, who had driven him all the day before (Jehu like), and that he had neither had corn, or hay, therefore

I was not to pay for the **horse—but** I might as well have whistled, **as have** spoke French, and I believe my **Latin was** equal to my uncle **Toby's** Lilabulero—being **not** understood because of **its purity, but by** dint of words I forced my judge to do me justice—no common thing, by the **way,** in France.—My wife and daughter are arrived—the latter does nothing but look out of the window, and complain of **the** torment of being frizled. —I wish she may ever remain a child of nature—I hate children of art.

I hope **this** will find your ladyship well—and that you will be kind enough **to** direct to me at Toulouse, which place I shall set out for very soon. I am, with truth and sincerity,

Your Ladyship's
Most faithful
L. Sterne.

Letter xxx.

To Mr E.

Paris, July 12, 1762.

Dear Sir,
My wife and daughter arrived here safe and sound **on** Thursday, and are in high raptures with the speed **and** pleasantness **of** their journey, and particularly of all **they** see and meet with here. But in their journey from York to Paris nothing has given them a more sensible and lasting pleasure, than the marks of kindness they received from you and Mrs E.—The friendship, good-will, and politeness of my two friends I never doubted to me, **or** mine, and I return you **both** all a grateful man is capable of, which is merely my thanks. I have taken, however, the liberty of sending an Indian taffety,

which Mrs E. must do me the honour to wear for my
wife's sake, who would have got it made up, but that
Mr Stanhope, the Consul of Algiers, who sets off to-
morrow morning for London, has been so kind (I
mean his lady) as to take charge of it; and we had
but just time to procure it: and had we missed that
opportunity, as we should have been obliged to have
left it behind us at Paris, we knew not when or how to
get it to our friend.—I wish it had been better worth
a paragraph. If there is any thing we can buy or
procure for you here (intelligence included), you have
a right to command me—for I am yours, with my wife
and girl's kind love to you and Mrs E.

LAU. STERNE.

Letter xxxi.

To J— H— S—, Esq.

My DEAR H.   Toulouse, August 12, 1762.

By the time you have got to the end of this long letter,
you will perceive that I have not been able to answer
your last till now—I have had the intention of doing it
almost as often as my prayers in my head—'tis thus we
use our best friends—What an infamous story is that
you have told me!—After some little remarks on it,
the rest of my letter will go on, like silk.   ****—is a
good-natured old easy fool, and has been deceived by
the most artful of her sex, and she must have abundance
of impudence and charlatanery, to have carried on such
a farce. I pity the old man for being taken in for so
much money—a man of sense I should have laughed
at—My wife saw her when in town, and she had not
the appearance of poverty; but when she wants to melt

****'s heart, she puts her gold watch and diamond
rings in her drawer.—But he might have been aware of
her.   I could not have been mistaken in her character
—and 'tis odd she should talk of her wealth to one,
and tell another the reverse—so good night to her—
About a week or ten days before my wife arrived at
Paris, I had the same accident I had at Cambridge, of
breaking a vessel in my lungs.   It happened in the
night, and I bled the bed full, and finding in the
morning I was likely to bleed to death, I sent immediately for a surgeon to bleed me at both arms—this
saved me, and, with lying speechless three days, I
recovered upon my back in bed; the breach healed,
and, in a week after, I got out—This, with my
weakness and hurrying about, made me think it high
time to haste to Toulouse.—We have had four months
of such heats that the oldest Frenchman never remem-
bers the like—'twas as hot as *Nebuchadnezzar's oven,*
and never has relaxed one hour—in the height of this,
'twas our destiny (or rather destruction) to set out by
way of Lyons, Montpellier, &c., to shorten, I trow, our
sufferings—Good God!—but 'tis over—and here I am
in my own house, quite settled by M—'s aid, and good-
natured offices, for which I owe him more than I can
express, or know how to pay at present—'Tis in the
prettiest situation in Toulouse, with near two acres of
garden—the house too good by half for us—well
furnished, for which I pay thirty pounds a year.—I
have got a good cook—my wife a decent *femme de
chambre,* and a good looking *laquais*—The Abbé has
planned our expences, and set us in such a train, we cannot easily go wrong—though by the bye, the d———l
is seldom found sleeping under a hedge.   Mr Trotter
dined with me the day before I left Paris—I took care
to see all executed according to your directions—but
Trotter, I dare say, by this, has wrote to you—I made

Crazy Castle.

him happy beyond expression with your Crazy Tales, and more so with its frontispiece.—I am in spirits, writing a crazy chapter—with my face turned towards thy turret—'Tis now I wish all warmer climates, countries, and every thing else, at ——, that separates me from our paternal seat—*ce sera là où reposera ma cendre—et ce sera là où mon cousin viendra repandre les pleurs dues à notre amitié.*—I am taking asses milk three times a day, and cows milk as often—I long to see thy face again once more—Greet the Colonel kindly in my name, and thank him cordially from me for his many civilities to Madame and Mademoiselle Shandy at York, who send all due acknowledgments. The humour is over for France, and Frenchmen, but that is not enough for your affectionate cousin,

L. S.

(A year will tire us all out, I trow) but thank Heaven the post brings me a letter from my Anthony —I felicitate you upon what Messrs the Reviewers allow you—they have too much judgment themselves not to allow you what you are actually possessed of, "talents, wit, and humour."—Well, write on, my dear cousin, and be guided by thy own fancy.—Oh! how I envy you all at Crazy Castle!—I could like to spend a month with you—and should return back again for the vintage.—I honour the man that has given the world an idea of our parental seat—'tis well done—I look at it ten times a day with a *quando te aspiciam ?*— Now farewell—remember me to my beloved Colonel— greet Panty most lovingly on my behalf, and if Mrs C—— and Miss C——, &c., are at G——, greet them likewise with a holy kiss—So GOD bless you.

𝔏𝔢𝔱𝔱𝔢𝔯 𝔵𝔵𝔵𝔦𝔦.

To Mr *Foley, at Paris.*

Toulouse, August 14, 1762.

MY DEAR FOLEY,

AFTER many turnings (*alias* digressions), to say nothing of downright overthrows, stops, and delays, we have arrived in three weeks at Toulouse, and are now settled in our houses with servants, &c., about us, and look as composed as if we had been here seven years.—In our journey we suffered so much from the heats, it gives me pain to remember it—I never saw a cloud from Paris to Nismes half as broad as a twenty-four sols piece.—Good GOD! we were toasted, roasted, grill'd, stew'd and carbonaded on one side or other all the way—and being all done enough (*assez cuits*) in the day, we were eat up at night by bugs, and other unswept out vermin, the legal inhabitants (if length of possession gives right) of every inn we lay at—Can you conceive a worse accident than that in such a journey, in the hottest day and hour of it, four miles from either tree or shrub which could cast a shade of the size of one of Eve's fig leaves—that we should break a hind wheel into ten thousand pieces, and be obliged in consequence to sit five hours on a gravelly road, without one drop of water, or possibility of getting any—To mend the matter, my two postillions were two dough-hearted fools, and fell a crying—Nothing was to be done! By heaven, quoth I, pulling off my coat and waistcoat, something shall be done, for I'll thrash you both within an inch of your lives—and then make you take each of you a horse, and ride like two devils to the next post for a cart to carry my baggage, and a wheel to carry ourselves—Our luggage weighed ten quintals—'twas the fair of Baucaire—all the world was going, or returning—we were ask'd by every soul who pass'd by us, if we were going to the fair of Baucaire— No wonder, quoth I, we have goods enough! *vous avez raison, mes amis.*

Well! here we are after all, my dear friend—and most deliciously placed at the extremity of the town, in an excellent house well furnish'd, and elegant beyond any thing I look'd for—'Tis built in the form of a hotel, with a pretty court towards the town—and behind, the best garden in Toulouse, laid out in serpentine walks, and so large, that the company in our quarter usually come to walk there in the evenings, for which they have my consent—" the more the merrier." —The house consists of a good *salle à manger* above stairs joining to the very great *salle à compagnie* as large as the Baron d'Holbach's; three handsome bedchambers with dressing rooms to them—below stairs two very good rooms for myself, one to study in, the other to see company.—I have moreover cellars round the court, and all other offices—Of the same landlord I have bargained to have the use of a country-house which he has two miles out of town, so that myself and all my family have nothing more to do than to take our hats and remove from the one to the other ——My landlord is moreover to keep the gardens in order and what do you think I am to pay for all this? neither more or less than thirty pounds a year—all things are cheap in proportion—so we shall live for very very little.—I dined yesterday with Mr H——; he is most pleasantly situated, and they are all well.— As for the books you have received for D——, the bookseller was a fool not to send the bill along with them—I will write to him about it.—I wish you was with me for two months; it would cure you of all evils ghostly and bodily—but this like many other wishes both for you and myself, must have its completion elsewhere—Adieu, my kind **friend, and** believe that I love you as much from inclination as reason, for

I am most truly **yours,**
L. STERNE.

My wife **and girl join** in compliments **to** you—My best respects to my worthy Baron d'Holbach and all that society—Remember me to my friend Mr Panchaud.

Letter xxxiij.

To J— H— S—, Esq.

MY DEAR H.   Toulouse, Oct. 19, 1762.

I RECEIVED **your** letter yesterday—**so it** has been travelling **from** Crazy Castle to Toulouse full eighteen days—If I had nothing to stop me I would engage to set out **this** morning, and knock at Crazy Castle gates in three days less time—by which time I should find you and the Colonel, Panty, &c., all alone—the season I **most** wish and like to be with you—I rejoice **from** my heart, down to my reins, that you have snatch'd **so** many happy and sunshiny days out of the hands of the blue devils—If we live to meet and join our forces as heretofore, we will give these gentry a drubbing—and turn them for **ever** out of their usurped citadel—some legions of **them** have been put to flight already by your operations **this** last campaign—and I hope to have a hand in dispersing the remainder **the** first time my dear cousin sets up his banners again under the square tower ———But what art thou meditating with axes and hammers?—"*I know the pride and the naughtiness of thy heart,*" and **thou** lovest the sweet visions of architraves, friezes and pediments with their tympanums, and thou hast found out a pretence, *à raison de cinq cent livres sterling* to be laid out in four years, &c. &c. (so as not to be felt, which is always added by the d———l as a bait) to justify thyself unto thyself—It may be very wise to do this—but 'tis wiser to keep one's money in one's pocket, whilst there are wars without and rumours of wars within. St ——— advises his disciples to sell both coat and waistcoat—and go rather without shirt or sword, than leave no money in their scrip to go to Jerusalem with—Now those *quatre ans consecutifs*, my dear Anthony, are the most precious morsels of thy *life to come* (in this world), and thou wilt do well to enjoy that morsel without cares, calculations, and curses, and damns, and debts—for as sure as stone is stone, and mortar is mortar, &c., 'twill be one of the many works of thy repentance—But after all, if the Fates have decreed it, as you and I have some time supposed it on account of your generosity, "*that you are never to be a monied man,*" the decree will be fulfilled whether you adorn your castle and line it with cedar, and paint it within side and without side with vermilion, or not—*et cela étant* (having a bottle of Frontiniac and glass at my right hand) I drink, dear Anthony, to thy health and happiness, and to the final accomplishments of all thy lunary and sublunary projects.—For six weeks together, after I wrote my last letter to you, my projects were many stories higher, for I was all that time, as I thought, journeying on to the other world—I fell ill of an epidemic vile fever which killed hundreds about me —The physicians here are the errantest charlatans in Europe, or the most ignorant of all pretending fools —I withdrew what was left of me out of their hands, and recommended my affairs entirely to Dame Nature —She (dear goddess), has saved me in fifty different pinching **bouts,** and I begin to **have a** kind of enthusiasm **now in** her **favour,** and in **my own, that** one or **two more** escapes **will make me believe I** shall leave you all **at last** by translation, and **not by** fair death. I am now stout **and** foolish again as a happy **man** can wish to be—and **am busy** playing the fool with **my** uncle Toby, whom **I** have got soused over head **and ears in** love.—**I have** many hints and projects for other works; all will **go on I** trust as I wish in this matter.—When I **have reaped** the benefit of this winter at **Toulouse—** I cannot **see** I have any thing more to do with it; **therefore** after having gone with my wife and girl to Bagnieres, I shall return **from** whence I came—— **Now my** wife **wants** to **stay another** year to **save** money, and this opposition **of wishes,** though it will **not be as sour as** lemon, **yet 'twill not be** as sweet as sugar-candy.—I wish T— would lead **Sir** Charles to Toulouse; **'tis as good** as any town **in the** South of France—for **my** own part, 'tis not to my taste—but I believe, the ground-work of my *ennui* is more to **the** eternal platitude **of the** French characters—little **variety, no** originality in it at all—than to any other cause—for they are very civil—but civility itself, **in** that uniform, wearies and bodders one to death—If I do not mind, I shall grow most stupid and sententious —Miss Shandy is hard at it with music, dancing, **and** French speaking, **in** the last of which she does *à merveille,* and **speaks** it with an excellent **accent,** considering she practises within sight **of** the Pyrenean Mountains.—If the snows will suffer **me, I** propose to spend two or three months at Barege, **or** Bagnieres, but my dear **wife** is against all **schemes** of additional expences—which wicked propensity (tho' not of despotic power) yet I cannot suffer—tho' by the bye laudable enough—But she may talk—I will do my **own** way, and she will acquiesce without **a** word of debate on the subject.—Who can say so much in praise of his wife? Few I trow.—M—— is out of town vintaging—so write to me, *Monsieur Sterne, gentilhomme Anglois*—'twill find me—We are as much out of the road of all intelligence here as at the Cape of Good Hope—so write a long nonsensical letter like this, now and then, to me—in which say nothing but what may be shewn, (tho' I love every paragraph and spirited stroke of your pen, others might not) for you must know, a letter no sooner arrives from England but curiosity is upon her knees to know the contents ——Adieu, dear H., believe me

Your affectionate
L. STERNE.

We have had bitter cold weather here these fourteen days—which has obliged us to sit with whole pagells of wood lighted up to our noses—'tis a dear article— but every thing else being extreme cheap, Madame keeps an excellent good house, with *soupe, bouilli, roti* —&c. &c., for two hundred and fifty pounds a year.

Letter xxxiv.

To Mr Foley, at Paris.

Toulouse, November 9, 1762.

MY DEAR FOLEY,

I HAVE had this week your letter on my table, and hope you will forgive my not answering it sooner—and even to-day I can but write you ten lines, being engaged at Mrs M—'s. I would not omit one post more acknowledging the favour—In a few posts I will write you a long one gratis, that is for love—Thank you for

having done what I desired **you**—**and** for the future
direct to me under **cover** at Monsieur Brousse's—I
receive all letters **through him** more punctual and sooner
than when left **at the post-house**———

H———'s family greet you **with** mine—we **are**
much together, and never forget you—forget me not to
the Baron—and all **the** circle—nor **to** your domestic
circle—

I **am** got pretty well, and sport much with my **uncle**
Toby in **the** volume I **am** now fabricating for **the**
laughing part of the world—for the melancholy part of it,
I have nothing but my prayers—so God help them.——
I shall hear from you in a post **or two at** least after you
receive this—in the mean time, **dear** Foley, adieu, and
believe no man wishes **or esteems** you more than
your

L. Sterne.

Letter xxxv.

To the same.

Toulouse, Wednesday, Dec. 3, 1762.

Dear Foley,

I **have** for this last fortnight every post-day **gone to**
Messrs B——— and Sons, in expectation of the pleasure
of a letter from you with the remittance I desired you
to send me here.——When a man has no more than half
a dozen guineas in his pocket—and **a** thousand miles
from home—and in a country, where he can as soon
raise the d—l, as **a** six livre piece **to** go to market
with in case he has changed his **last** guinea—you will
not envy my situation—God bless you—remit me the
balance due upon the receipt **of** this.——We are all at
H—'s, practising a play we are to act here this Christ-

mas holidays—all the Dramatis Personæ are of the English, of which we have a happy society living together like brothers and sisters—Your banker here has just sent me word the tea Mr H. wrote for is to be delivered into my hands—'tis all one into whose hands the treasure falls—we shall pay Brousse for it the day we get it—We join in our most friendly respects, and believe me, dear Foley, truly yours,

L. Sterne.

Letter xxxvi.

To the same.

Toulouse, Dec. 17, 1762.

My dear Foley,

The post after I wrote last, I received yours with the inclosed draught upon the receiver, for which I return you all thanks—I have received this day likewise the box and tea all safe and sound—so we shall all of us be in our cups this Christmas, and drink without fear or stint.—We begin to live extremely happy, and are all together every night—fiddling, laughing and singing, and cracking jokes. You will scarce believe the news I tell you—There are a company of English strollers arrived here, who are to act comedies all the Christmas, and are now busy in making dresses, and preparing some of our best comedies—Your wonder will cease, when I inform you these strollers are your friends with the rest of our society, to whom I proposed this scheme *soulagement*—and I assure you we do well.—The next week, with a grand orchestra, we play the Busy Body—and the Journey to London the week after; but I have some thoughts of adapting it to our situation—and making it the Journey to Toulouse, which, with the change of half a dozen scenes, may be easily done.—Thus, my dear F., for want of something better we have recourse to ourselves, and strike out the best amusements we can from such materials.—My kind love and friendship to all my true friends—My service to the rest. H——'s family have just left me, having been this last week with us, —they will be with me all the holidays.—In summer we shall visit them, and so balance hospitalities.

.   Adieu,

Yours most truly,

L. STERNE.

Letter xxxvii.

To the same.

Toulouse, March 29, 1763.

DEAR FOLEY,

—THOUGH that's a mistake! I mean the date of the place, for I write at Mr H——'s in the country, and have been there with my people all the week—" How does Tristram do?" you say in yours to him—faith but so so—the worst of human maladies is poverty— though that is a second lie—for poverty of spirit is worse than poverty of purse by ten thousand per cent. —I inclose you a remedy for the one, a draught of a hundred and thirty pounds, for which I insist upon a rescription by the very return—or I will send you and all your commissaries to the d——l.—I do not hear they have tasted of one fleshy banquet all this Lent— you will make an excellent *grillé*, P— they can make nothing of him, but *bouillon*—I mean my other two friends no ill—so shall send them a reprieve as they acted out of necessity—not choice—My kind respects to Baron d'Holbach, and all his household—Say all that's kind for me to my other friends—you know how much, dear Foley, I am yours,

L. STERNE.

I have not five Louis to vapour with in this land of coxcombs—My wife's compliments.

Letter xxxviii.

To the same.

DEAR FOLEY,   Toulouse, April 18, 1763.

I THANK you for your punctuality in sending me the rescription, and for your box by the courier, which came safe by last post.—I was not surprised much with your account of Lord ***** being obliged to give way—and for the rest, all follows in course.—I suppose you will endeavour to fish and catch something for yourself in these troubled waters—at least I wish you all a reasonable man can wish for himself—which is wishing enough for you—all the rest is in the brain —Mr Woodhouse (whom you know) is also here— he is a most amiable worthy man, and I have the pleasure of having him much with me—in a short time he proceeds to Italy.—The first week in June, I decamp like a patriarch with my whole household, to pitch our tents for three months at the foot of the Pyrenean Hills at Bagnieres, where I expect much health and much amusement from the concourse of adventurers from all corners of the earth.—Mrs

M—— sets out, at the same time, for another part of
the Pyrenean Hills, at Courtray—from whence to
Italy—This is the general plan of operation here—except that I have some thoughts of spending the winter
at Florence, and crossing over with my family to
Leghorn by water—and in April of returning by way
of Paris home—but this is a sketch only, for in all
things I am governed by circumstances—so that what
is fit to be done on Monday, may be very unwise on
Saturday—On all days of the week, believe me yours,

With unfeigned truth,
L. STERNE.

P.S.—All compliments to my Parisian friends.

Letter xxxix.

To the same.

My DEAR FOLEY,   Toulouse, April 29, 1763.

LAST post my agent wrote me word he would send up
from York a bill for fourscore guineas, with orders to
be paid into Mr Selwin's hands for me. This he said
he would expedite immediately, so 'tis possible you
may have had advice of it—and 'tis possible also the
money may not be paid this fortnight; therefore, as I
set out for Bagnieres in that time, be so good as to give
me credit for the money for a few posts or so, and send
me either a rescription for the money, or a draught for
it—at the receipt of which, we shall decamp for ten or
twelve weeks—You will receive twenty pounds more
on my account, which send also—So much for that—

as for pleasure—you have it all amongst you at Paris—
we have nothing here which deserves the name—I shall
scarce be tempted to sojourn another winter in Toulouse
—for I cannot say it suits my health as I hoped—'tis
too moist—and I cannot keep clear of agues here—so
that if I stay the next winter on this side of the water
—'twill be either at Nice or Florence—and I shall
return to England in April—Wherever I am, believe
me, dear Foley, that I am

Yours faithfully,

L. STERNE.

Madame and Mademoiselle present their best compliments—Remember me to all I regard, particularly
Messrs Panchaud, and the rest of your *household.*

Letter ɼl.

To the same.

Toulouse, May 21, 1763.

I TOOK the liberty, three weeks ago, to desire you
would be so kind as to send me fourscore pounds,
having received a letter the same post from my
agent, that he would order. the money to be paid to
your correspondent in London in a fortnight.—It is
some disappointment to me that you have taken no
notice of my letter, especially as I told you we waited
for the money before we set out for Bagnieres—and so
little distrust had I that such a civility would be refused
me, that we have actually had all our things packed up
these eight days, in hourly expectation of receiving a
letter.—Perhaps my good friend has waited till he
heard the money was paid in London—but you might

have trusted to my honour—that all the cash in your **iron box** (and all the bankers in Europe put together) **could not** have tempted me to **say the** thing *that is not.* —I hope before this you will have received an account of the money being paid in **London—But it** would have been taken kindly, if you had wrote me word you would transmit me the money when you had received it, but no sooner ; for Mr R— of Montpellier, though I know him not, yet knows enough of me to have given me credit for a fortnight for ten times the sum.

I am, dear **F—,** your friend
and hearty well-wisher,
L. Sterne.

I saw the family of the **H——** yesterday, and asked them if you was **in the** land of the living—They said yea—for they had just **received** a letter **from** you.— After all, **I** heartily forgive you—for you have done me a signal service **in** mortifying **me, and** it **is this,** I am determined **to** grow rich **upon it.**

Adieu, and God send you wealth and happiness— All compliments to —. Before April next I am obliged to revisit your metropolis in my **way** to England.

———

Letter xli.

To the same.

Toulouse, June 9, 1763.

My dear Foley,
I this moment received yours—consequently the moment I got it I sat down **to** answer it—So much for a logical inference.

Now believe me I had never wrote you so testy a letter, had I not both loved and esteemed you—and it was merely in vindication of the rights of friendship that I wrote in a way as if I was hurt—for neglect me in your heart, I knew you could not, without cause; which my heart told me I never had—or will ever give you:—I was the best friends with you that ever I was in my life, before my letter had got a league, and pleaded the true excuse for my friend, "That he was oppressed with a multitude of business." Go on, my dear F., and have but that excuse (so much do I regard your interest), that I would be content to suffer a *real evil* without future murmuring—but in truth, my disappointment was partly chimerical at the bottom, having a letter of credit for two hundred pounds from a person I never saw, by me—but which, out of a nicety of temper, I would not make any use of—I set out in two days for Bagnieres, but direct to me to Brousse, who will forward all my letters.—Dear F—, adieu.—Believe me

Yours affectionately,
L. STERNE.

Letter xlij.

To the same.

DEAR FOLEY,   Toulouse, June 12, 1763.

LUCKILY just before I was stepping into my chaise for Bagnieres, has a strayed fifty pound bill found its way to me; so I have sent it to its lawful owner inclosed—My noodle of an agent, instead of getting Mr Selwin to advise you he had received the money (which would have been enough), has got a bill for it, and

sent it rambling to the furthest part of France after
me; and if it had not caught me just now, it might
have followed me into Spain, for I shall cross the
Pyreneans, and spend a week in that kingdom, which
is enough for a fertile brain to write a volume upon.—
When I write the history of my travels — Memorandum! I am not to forget how honest a man I
have for a banker at Paris.—But, my dear friend, when
you say you dare trust me for what little occasions I
may have, you have as much faith as honesty—and
more of both than of good policy. — I thank you
however ten thousand times—and except such liberty
as I have lately taken with you—and that too at a
pinch—I say beyond that I will not trespass upon
your good-nature, or friendliness, to serve me.—God
bless you, dear F—,

I am yours whilst

L. Sterne.

Letter xliij.

To the same.

Dear Foley,   Montpellier, Oct. 5, 1763.

I am ashamed I have not taken an opportunity of thank-
ing you before now, for your friendly act of civility, in
ordering Brousse, your correspondent at Toulouse, in
case I should have occasion, to pay me fifteen hundred
livres—which, as I knew the offer came from your
heart, I made no difficulty of accepting.—In my way
through Toulouse to Marseilles, where we have been,
but neither liking the place nor Aix (particularly the
latter, it being a parliament town, of which Toulouse has

given me a surfeit), we have returned here, where we shall reside the winter—My wife and daughter purpose to stay a year at least behind me; and when winter is over, to return to Toulouse, or go to Montauban, where they will stay till they return, or I fetch them—For myself, I shall set out in February for England, where my heart has been fled these six months—but I shall stay a fortnight with my friends at Paris; though I verily believe, if it was not for the pleasure of seeing and chattering with you, I should pass on directly to Brussels, and so on to Rotterdam, for the sake of seeing Holland, and embark from thence to London—But I must stay a little with those I love and have so many reasons to regard—you cannot place too much of this to your own score.—I have had an offer of going to Italy a fortnight ago—but I must like my subject as well as the terms, neither of which were to my mind. —Pray what English have you at Paris? where is my young friend Mr F—? We hear of three or four English families coming to us here—If I can be serviceable to any you would serve, you have but to write.—Mr H—— has sent my friend W—'s picture —You have seen the original, or I would have sent it you—I believe I shall beg leave to get a copy of my own from yours, when I come *in propria persona*—till when, God bless you, my dear friend, and believe me

Most faithfully yours,
L. Sterne.

Letter xliv.

To the same.

My dear Friend,   Montpellier, Jan. 5, 1764.

You see I cannot pass over the fifth of the month
without thinking of you, and writing to you—The last
is a periodical habit—the first is from my heart, and
I do it oftner than I remember—however, from both
motives together I maintain I have a right to the
pleasure of a single line—be it only to tell me how
your watch goes—You know how much happier it
would make me to know that all things belonging to
you went on well.—You are going to have them all to
yourself (I hear), and that Mr S—— is true to his
first intention of leaving business—I hope this will
enable you to accomplish yours in a shorter time, that
you may get to your long-wished-for retreat of tran-
quillity and silence—When you have got to your fire-
side, and into your arm-chair (and, by the bye, have
another to spare for a friend), and are so much a
sovereign, as to sit in your furred cap, if you like it,
though I should not (for a man's ideas are at least the
cleaner for being dressed decently), why then it will
be a miracle if I do not glide in like a ghost upon you
—and in a very unghostlike fashion help you off with
a bottle of your best wine.

January 15.—It does not happen every day that a
letter begun in the most perfect health, should be concluded in the greatest weakness—I wish the vulgar
high and low do not say it was a judgment upon me,
for taking all this liberty with *ghosts*—Be it as it may
—I took a ride, when the first part of this was wrote,
towards Pezenas—and returned home in a shivering fit,

though I ought to have been in a fever, for I had tired my beast; and he was as unmoveable as Don Quixotte's wooden horse, and my arm was half dislocated in whipping him—This, quoth I, is inhuman—No, says a peasant on foot behind me, I'll drive him home— so he laid on his posteriors, but 'twas needless—as his face was turned towards Montpellier, he began to trot.—But to return, this fever has confined me ten days in my bed—I have suffered in this scuffle with death terribly—but unless the spirit of prophecy deceive me—I shall not die but live—in the mean time, dear F., let us live as merrily, but *as innocently* as we can— It has ever been as good, if not better, than a bishop-rick to me—and *I desire no other*—Adieu, my dear friend, and believe me yours,

L. S.

Please to give the inclosed to Mr T——, and tell him I thank him cordially from my heart for his great *good-will.*

Letter xlv.

To the same.

Montpellier, Jan. 20 [1764].

My dear Friend,

Hearing by Lord Rochford (who in passing thro' here in his way to Madrid has given me a call), that my worthy friend Mr Fox was now at Paris—I have inclosed a letter to him, which you will present in course, or direct to him.—I suppose you are full of English—but in short we are here as if in another world, where unless some stray'd soul arrives, we know nothing of what is going on in yours—Lord G————r

I suppose is gone from Paris, or I had wrote also to him. I know you are as busy as a bee, and have few moments to yourself—nevertheless bestow one of them upon an old friend, and write me a line—and if Mr F. is too idle, and has ought to say to me, pray write a second line for him—We had a letter from Miss P——— this week, who it seems has decamp'd for ever from Paris—*All is for the best*—which is my general reflection upon many things in this world—Well! I shall shortly come and shake you by the hand in St Sauveur —if still you are there.—My wife returns to Toulouse, and purposes to spend the summer at Bagnieres—I on the contrary go and visit my wife, the church in Yorkshire.—We all live the longer—at least the happier, for having things our own way.—This is my conjugal maxim —I own 'tis not the best of maxims—but I maintain 'tis not the worst. Adieu, dear F———, and believe me

Yours with truth,

L. Sterne.

Letter xlvi.

To Mrs F.

Montpellier, Feb. 1, 1764.

I am preparing, my dear Mrs F., to leave France, for I am heartily tired of it—That insipidity there is in French characters has disgusted your friend Yorick.— I have been dangerously ill, and cannot think that the sharp air of Montpellier has been of service to me— and so my physicians told me when they had me under their hands for above a month—if you stay any longer here, Sir, it will be fatal to you—And why, good people, were you not kind enough to tell me this sooner?—After having discharged them, I told Mrs Sterne that I should set out for England very soon; but as she chuses to remain in France for two or three years, I have no objection, except that I wish my girl in England.—The states of Languedoc are met—'tis a fine raree-shew, with the usual accompaniments of fiddles, bears, and puppet-shews.—I believe I shall step into my post-chaise with more alacrity to fly from these sights, than a Frenchman would to fly to them—and except a tear at parting with my little slut, I shall be in high spirits; and every step I take that brings me nearer England, will I think help to set this poor frame to rights. Now pray write to me, directed to Mr F. at Paris, and tell me, what I am to bring you over.—How do I long to greet all my friends! few do I value more than yourself.—My wife chuses to go to Montauban, rather than stay here, in which I am truly passive.—If this should not find you at Bath, I hope it will be forwarded to you, as I wish to fulfil your commissions—and so adieu—Accept every warm wish for your health, and believe me ever yours,

L. STERNE.

P.S.—My physicians have almost poisoned me with what they call *bouillons refraichissants*—'tis a cock flayed alive and boiled with poppy seeds, then pounded in a mortar, afterwards pass'd thro' a sieve—There is to be one crawfish in it, and I was gravely told it must be a male one—a female would do me more hurt than good.

L

G

Letter xlvii.

To *Miss Sterne.*

Paris, May 15, 1764.

MY DEAR LYDIA,

BY this time I suppose your mother and self are fixed at Montauban, and I therefore direct to your banker, to be delivered to you.—I acquiesced in your staying in France—likewise it was your mother's wish—but I must tell you both (that unless your health had not been a plea made use of) I should have wished you both to return with me.—I have sent you the Spectators, and other books, particularly Metastasio; but I beg my girl to read the former, and only make the latter her amusement.—I hope you have not forgot my last request, to make no friendships with the French women—not that I think ill of them all, but sometimes women of the best principles are the most *insinuating*—nay I am so jealous of you, that I should be miserable were I to see you had the least grain of coquetry in your composition.—You have enough to do—for I have also sent you a guittar—and as you have no genius for drawing (tho' you never could be made to believe it), pray waste not your time about it —Remember to write to me as to a friend—in short, whatever comes into your little head, and then it will be natural.—If your mother's rheumatism continues, and she chooses to go to Bagnieres, tell her not to be stopped for want of money, for my purse shall be as open as my heart. I have preached at the Ambassador's chapel—Hezekiah *— (an odd subject your mother will say). There was a concourse of all nations, and religions too.—I shall leave Paris in a few days—I am lodged in the same hotel with Mr T——; they are

* See this Sermon, *post.*

good and generous souls—Tell your mother that I hope she will write to me, and that when she does so, I may also receive a letter from my Lydia.

Kiss your mother from me, and believe me

Your affectionate
L. STERNE.

————

Letter xlviij.

To Mr Foley.

York, August 6, 1764.

MY DEAR FOLEY,

THERE is a young lady with whom I have sent a letter to you, who will arrive at Paris in her way to Italy— her name is Miss Tuting; a lady known and loved by the whole kingdom—if you can be of any aid to her in your advice, &c., as to her journey, &c., your good nature and politeness I am sure need no spur from me to do it. I was sorry we were like the two buckets of a well, whilst in London, for we were never able to be both resident together the month I continued in and about the environs.———If I get a cough this winter which holds me three days, you will certainly see me at Paris the week following, for now I abandon every thing in this world to health and to my friends—for the last sermon that I shall ever preach, was preach'd at Paris—so I am altogether an idle man, or rather a free one, which is better. I sent, last post, twenty pounds to Mrs Sterne, which makes a hundred pounds remitted since I got here.—You must pay yourself what I owe you out of it—and place the rest to account. —Betwixt this and Lady-day next, Mrs Sterne will draw from time to time upon you to about the amount of a hundred louis—but not more—(I think) I having left her a hundred in her pocket.—But you shall always have money beforehand of mine—and she purposes to spend no further than five thousand livres in the year —but twenty pounds this way or that, makes no difference between us.——Give my kindest compliments to Mr P——. I have a thousand things to say to you, and would go half way to Paris to tell them you in your ear.—The Messrs T——, H——, &c., and many more of your friends with whom I am now, send their services—Mine to all friends—Yours, dear F., most truly,

L. STERNE.

Letter rlir.

To J— H— S—, Esq.

September 4, 1764.

Now, my dear, dear Anthony—I do not think a week or ten days playing the good fellow (at this very time) at Scarborough so abominable a thing—but if a man could get there cleverly, and every soul in his house in the mind to try what could be done in furtherance thereof, I have no one to consult in this affair—therefore as a man may do worse things, the English of all which is this, that I am going to leave a few poor sheep here in the wilderness for fourteen days—and from pride and naughtiness of heart to go see what is doing at Scarborough—stedfastly meaning afterwards to lead a new life and strengthen my faith.—Now some folk say there is much company there—and some say not—and I believe there is neither the one or the other—but will be both, if the world will have but a month's patience or so.—No, my dear H——, I did not delay sending your letter directly to the post.—As there are critical times, or rather turns and revolutions in *** humours, I knew not what the delay of an hour might hazard— I will answer for him, he has seventy times seven forgiven you—and as often wish'd you at the d—l.— After many oscillations the pendulum will rest firm as ever.———

I send all kind compliments to Sir C. D—— and G—s. I love them from my soul.—If G——t is with you, him also.—I go on, not rapidly, but well enough with my uncle Toby's amours—There is no sitting, and cudgelling one's brains whilst the sun shines bright—'twill be all over in six or seven weeks, and there are dismal months enow after to endure suffocation by a brimstone fire-side.—If you can get to Scarborough do.—A man who makes six tons of alum a week, may do any thing—Lord Granby is to be there———what a temptation!

Yours affectionately,
L. STERNE.

Letter L.

To the same.

Coxwould—Thursday [Sept. 1764].

MY DEAR COUSIN,

I AM but this moment returned from Scarborough, where I have been drinking the waters ever since the races, and have received marvellous strength, had I not debilitated it as fast as I got it, by playing the good fellow with Lord Granby and Co. too much. I rejoice you have been encamp'd at Harrowgate, from which, by now, I suppose you are decamp'd—

otherwise as idle a beast as I have been, I would
have sacrificed a few days to the god of laughter with
you and your jolly set.—I have done nothing good
that I know of, since I left you, except paying off your
guinea and a half to K——, in my way thro' York
hither—I must try now and do better—Go on, and
prosper for a month.

Your affectionate
L. STERNE.

Letter li.

To Mr *Foley*, at Paris.

York, September 29, 1764.

MY DEAR FRIEND,
I HAVING just had the honour of a letter from Miss
Tuting, full of the acknowledgments of your attention
and kind services to her; I will not believe these arose
from the D. of A——'s letters, nor mine. Surely
she needed no recommendation——the truest and most
honest compliment I can pay you, is to say they came
from your own good heart, only you was introduced
to the object—for the rest follow'd in course—However let me cast in my mite of thanks to the treasury
which belongs to good-natured actions. I have been
with Lord G—y these three weeks at Scarborough—
the pleasures of which I found somewhat more exalted
than those of Bagnieres last year.—I am now returned
to my Philosophical Hut to finish Tristram, which I
calculate will be ready for the world about Christmas,
at which time I decamp from hence, and fix my head-
quarters at London for the winter—unless my cough
pushes me forwards to your Metropolis—or that I can

persuade some *gros* my Lord to take a trip to you—
I'll try if I can make him relish the joys of the *Tuilleries*,
Opera Comique, &c.

I had this week a letter from Mrs Sterne from
Montauban, in which she tells me she has occasion
for fifty pounds immediately—Will you send an order
to your correspondent at Montauban to pay her so
much cash—and I will in three weeks send as much
to Becket—But as her purse is low, for God's sake
write directly.—Now you must do something equally
essential—to rectify a mistake in the mind of your
correspondent there, who it seems gave her a hint not
long ago, "*that she was separated from me for life*"—
Now as this is not true in the first place, and may give
a disadvantageous impression of her to those she lives
amongst——'twould be unmerciful to let her, or my
daughter, suffer by it;—so do be so good as to un-
deceive him—for in a year or two she proposes (and
indeed I expect it with impatience from her) to rejoin
me—and tell them I have all the confidence in the
world she will not spend more than I can afford, and
I only mentioned two hundred guineas a year—because
'twas right to name some certain sum, for which I
begged you to give her credit.—I write to you of all
my most intimate concerns, as to a brother; so excuse
me, dear Foley.   God bless you—Believe me

Yours affectionately,
L. STERNE.

Compliments to Mr Panchaud, D'Holbach, &c.

Letter lij.

To the same.

York, November 11, 1764.

My dear Friend,

I sent ten days ago, a bank bill of thirty pounds to Mr Becket, and this post one of sixty—When I get to London, which will be in five weeks, you will receive what shall always keep you in bank for Mrs Sterne; in the mean time I have desired Becket to send you fourscore pounds, and if my wife, before I get to London, should have occasion for fifty louis, let her not wait a minute, and if I have not paid it, a week or a fortnight I know will break no squares with a good and worthy friend.——I will contrive to send you these two new volumes of Tristram, as soon as ever I get them from the press.—You will read as odd a tour through France as ever was projected or executed by traveller, or travel-writers, since the world began—'Tis a laughing good-tempered satire against travelling (as *puppies* travel)—Panchaud will enjoy it—I am quite civil to your Parisians—*et pour cause* you know—'tis likely I may see them in spring—Is it possible for you to get me over a copy of my picture any how? If so, I would write to Mademoiselle N—— to make as good a copy from it as she possibly could—with a view to do her service here—and I would remit her the price—I really believe it would be the parent of a dozen portraits to her, if she executes it with the spirit of the original in your hands—for it will be seen by many—and as my phiz is as remarkable as myself, if she preserves the true character of both, it will do her honour and service too. —Write me a line about this, and tell me you are well and happy—Will you present my kind respects to the worthy Baron—I shall send him one of the best impressions of my picture from Mr Reynolds's—another to Monsieur P———. My love to Mr S———n and P——d.

I am most truly yours,
L. STERNE.

Letter liii.

To J— H— S—, Esq.

Nov. 13, 1764.

DEAR, DEAR COUSIN,

'TIS a church militant week with me, full of marches, and countermarches—and treaties about Stillington common, which we are going to inclose—otherwise I would have obeyed your summons—and yet I could not well have done it this week neither, having received a letter from C—, who has been very ill; and is coming down to stay a week or ten days with me—Now I know he is ambitious of being better acquainted with you; and longs from his soul for a sight of you in your own castle. I cannot do otherwise than bring him with me—nor can I gallop away and leave him an empty house to pay a visit to from London, as he comes half express to see me.— I thank you for the care of my northern vintage—I fear after all I must give it a fermentation on the other side of the Alps, which is better than being on the lees with it—but *nous verrons*—yet I fear as it has got such hold of my brain, and comes upon it like an armed man at nights—I must give way for quietness sake, or be hag-ridden with the conceit of it all my life long—I have been *Miss-ridden* this last week by a couple of romping girls (*bien mises et comme il faut*) who might as well have been in the house with me (though perhaps not, my retreat here is too quiet for them), but they

have taken up all my time, and **have** given **my** judgment
and fancy **more** airings **than** they wanted.—These
things accord **not** well **with** sermon-making—but 'tis
my vile errantry, as Sancho says, and **that is** all that
can be made **of it.—I trust** all goes swimmingly on
with your alum; **that the** works amuse you, and call
you twice out (at least) **a** day.—I shall **see** them I
trust in **ten** days, or thereabouts—If it was any **way**
possible, **I** would set out this moment, though I **have**
no cavalry—(*except a she Ass*). Give all friendly **re-**
spects to Mrs C. and to Col. H—'s, and the garrison,
both of Guisbro and Skelton.—I am, dear Anthony,

Affectionately yours,
L. Sterne.

Letter liv.

To Mr Foley, at P.

York, November 16, 1764.

My dear Friend,
Three posts before I had the favour of yours (which
is come to hand this moment) I had wrote to set Mrs
Sterne right in her mistake—That you had any money
of mine in your hands—being very sensible that the
hundred pounds I had sent you, through Becket's hands,
was but **about what** would balance with you—The
reason of her **error** was owing to my writing her word,
I would send you a bill in a post or two for fifty pounds
—which, my finances falling short just then, I deferred
—**so** that I had paid nothing **to** any one—but was,
however, come to York this day, **and** I have sent you a
draught for a hundred pounds—in honest truth, a fortnight ago I had not the cash—but I am as honest as the
king (as Sancho Panca says), *only not so rich.*

Therefore if Mrs Sterne should want thirty louis more, let her have them—and I will balance all (which will not be much) with honour at Christmas, when I shall be in London, having now just finished my two volumes of Tristram.—I have some thoughts of going to Italy this year—at least I shall not defer it above another.——I have been with Lord Granby, and with Lord Shelburne, but am now sat down till December in my sweet retirement.—I wish you was sat down as happily, and as free of all worldly cares——In a few years, my dear F., I hope to see you a real country gentleman, though not altogether exiled from your friends in London—there I shall spend every winter of my life, in the same lap of contentment, where I enjoy myself now—and wherever I go—we must bring three parts in four of the treat along with us—In short, we must be happy within—and then few things without us make much difference—This is my Shandean philosophy.—You will read a comic account of my journey from Calais, through Paris, to the Garonne, in these volumes—my friends tell me they are done with spirit——it must speak for itself—Give my kind respects to Mr Selwin and my friend Panchaud—— When you see Baron d'Holbach, present him my respects, and believe me, dear F.,

Yours cordially,
L. STERNE.

Letter lb.

To David Garrick, Esq.

London, March 16, 1765.

DEAR GARRICK,

I THREATENED you with a letter in one I wrote a few weeks ago to Foley, but (to my shame be it spoken) I lead such a life of dissipation I have never had a moment to myself which has not been broke in upon, by one engagement or impertinence or another—and as plots thicken towards the latter end of a piece, I find, unless I take pen and ink just now, I shall not be able to do it, till either I am got into the country, or you to the city.   You are teized and tormented too much by your correspondents, to return to us, and with accounts how much your friends, and how much your Theatre wants you—so that I will not magnify either our loss or yours—but hope cordially to see you soon.——Since I wrote last I have frequently stept into your house—that is, as frequently as I could take the whole party, where I dined, along with me—This was but justice to you, as I walked in as a wit—but with regard to myself, I balanced the account thus—I am sometimes in my friend ———'s house, but he is always in Tristram Shandy's—where my friends say he will continue (and I hope the prophecy true for my own immortality), even when he himself is no more.

I have had a lucrative winter's campaign here—Shandy sells well—I am taxing the public with two more volumes of Sermons, which will more than double the gains of Shandy—It goes into the world with a prancing list *de toute la noblesse*—which will bring me in three hundred pounds, exclusive of the sale of the copy—so that with all the contempt of money which *ma façon de penser* has ever impressed on me, I shall be rich in spite of myself : but I scorn, you must know, in the high *ton* I take at present, to pocket all this trash—I set out to lay a portion of it out in the service of the world, in a tour round Italy, where I shall spring game, or the deuce is in the dice.—In the beginning of September I quit England, that I may avail myself of the time of vintage, when all nature is joyous, and so saunter philosophically for a year or so, on the other side the Alps.—I hope your pilgrimages have brought Mrs Garrick and yourself back *à la fleur de jeunesse*—May you both long feel the sweets of it, and your friends with you.—Do, dear friend, make my kindest wishes and compliments acceptable to the best and wisest of the daughters of Eve—You shall ever believe, and ever find me affectionately yours,

L. STERNE.

Letter lvi.

To the same.

Bath, April 6, 1765.

I SCALP you!—my dear Garrick! my dear friend! foul befal the man who hurts a hair of your head!— and so full was I of that very sentiment, that my letter had not been put into the post-office ten minutes, before my heart smote me; and I sent to recal it—but failed —You are sadly to blame, Shandy! for this, quoth I, leaning with my head on my hand, as I recriminated upon my false delicacy in the affair—Garrick's nerves (if he has any left) are as fine and delicately spun as thy own—his sentiments as honest and friendly—thou knowest, Shandy, that he loves thee—why wilt thou hazard him a moment's pain? Puppy! fool, coxcomb,

jack-ass, &c. &c.—and so I balanced the account to
your favour, before I received it drawn up in *your way*
—I say *your way*—for it is not stated so much to your
honour and credit, as I had passed the account before
—for it was a most lamented truth, that I never received one of the letters your friendship meant me,
except whilst in Paris—Oh! how I congratulate you
for the anxiety the world has, and continues to be
under, for your return.—Return, return to the few who
love you, and the thousands who admire you.—The
moment you set your foot upon your stage—mark! I
tell it you—by some magic irresisted power, every fibre
about your heart will vibrate afresh, and as strong and
feelingly as ever—Nature, with glory at her back, will
light up the torch within you—and there is enough of
it left, to heat and enlighten the world these many,
many, many years.

Heaven be praised! (I utter it from my soul) that
your lady, and my Minerva, is in a condition to walk
to Windsor—full rapturously will I lead the graceful
pilgrim to the temple, where I will sacrifice with the
purest incense to her—but you may worship with me,
or not—'twill make no difference either in the truth or
warmth of my devotion—still (after all I have seen) I
still maintain her peerless.

Powel! good Heaven!—give me some one with less
smoke and more fire—There are who, like the Phari-
sees, still think they shall be heard for *much* speaking
—Come—come away, my dear Garrick, and teach us
another lesson.

Adieu!—I love you dearly—and your lady better
—not hobbihorsically—but most sentimentally and
affectionately—for I am yours (that is, if you never say
another word about ——) with all the sentiments of
love and friendship you deserve from me,

                                    L. STERNE.

Letter lvij.

To Mr Foley.

My dear Foley,   Bath, April 15, 1765.

My wife tells me she has drawn for one hundred pounds, and 'tis fit that you should be paid it that minute—the money is now in Becket's hands—send me, my dear Foley, my account, that I may discharge the balance to this time, and know what to leave in your hands—I have made a good campaign of it this year in the field of the literati—my two volumes of Tristram, and two of Sermons, which I shall print very soon, will bring me a considerable sum.—Almost all the nobility in England honour me with their names, and 'tis thought it will be the largest and most splendid list which ever pranced before a book, since subscriptions came into fashion.—Pray present my most sincere compliments to Lady H——, whose name I hope to insert with many others.—As so many men of genius favour me with their names also, I will quarrel with Mr Hume, and call him Deist, and what not, unless I have his name too.—My love to Lord W——. Your name, Foley, I have put in as a free-will offering of my labours—your list of subscribers you will send— 'tis but a crown for sixteen sermons—Dog cheap! but I am in quest of honour, not money.—Adieu, adieu,— believe me, dear Foley,

Yours truly,
L. Sterne.

Letter lviij.

To Mr W.

Coxwould, May **23,** 1765.

At this moment I am sitting in my summer-house
with my head and heart full, not of my uncle Toby's
amours with the widow Wadman, but my sermons—
and your letter has drawn me out of a pensive mood—the
spirit of it *pleaseth me*—but in this solitude, what **can** I
tell **or write to** you but about myself—I am glad that
you are in love—'twill cure you at least of the spleen,
which has a bad effect on both **man** and woman—I
myself must ever have some Dulcinea **in my** head—it
harmonises the soul—and in those cases **I first** endeavour
to make the lady believe so, or rather **I begin first to**
make myself believe that I am in **love—but I** carry on
my affairs quite **in the** French **way,** sentimentally—
"*l'amour*" (say they) "*n'est rien sans sentiment*"—Now
notwithstanding they make such a pother about the
word, they have no precise idea annex'd to it—And
so much for that same subject called love.—I must tell
you how I have just treated a French gentleman **of**
fortune in France, who took a liking to my daughter—
Without any ceremony (having got my direction from
my wife's banker) he wrote me word that he was in
love with my daughter, and desired to know what
fortune I would give her at present, and how much at
my *death*—by the bye, I think there **was** very little
sentiment on *his side*—My **answer** was, "Sir, I shall
give her ten thousand pounds **the day** of marriage—my
calculation is **as** follows—she **is not** eighteen, you are
sixty-two—there goes five thousand pounds—then, Sir,
you **at** least think her not ugly—she has many accomplishments, speaks Italian, French, plays upon the

guittar, and as I fear you play upon no instrument whatever, I think you will be happy to take her at my terms, for here finishes the account of the ten thousand pounds "—I do not suppose but he will take this as I mean, that is—a flat refusal.—I have had a parsonage house burnt down by the carelessness of my curate's wife—as soon as I can I must rebuild it, I trow—but I lack the means at present—yet I am never happier than when I have not a shilling in my pocket—for when I have I can never call it my own.—Adieu, my dear friend—may you enjoy better health than me, tho' not better spirits, for that is impossible.

Yours sincerely,
L. STERNE.

My compliments to the Col.

Letter lix.

To Mr Foley, at Paris.

MY DEAR SIR,   York, July 13. 1765.

I WROTE some time in spring, to beg you would favour me with my account. I believe you was set out from Paris, and that Mr Garrick brought the letter with him —which possibly he gave you. In the hurry of your business you might forget the contents of it; and in the hurry of mine in town (though I called once) I could not get to see you. I decamp for Italy in September, and shall see your face at Paris, you may be sure—but I shall see it with more pleasure when I am out of debt —which is your own fault, for Becket has had money left in his hands for that purpose.—Do send Mrs Sterne

I.   H

her two last volumes of Tristram; they arrived with yours in Spring, and she complains she has not got them—My best services to Mr Panchaud.—I am busy composing two volumes of sermons—they will be printed in September, though I fear not time enough to bring them with me.   Your name is amongst the list of a few of my honorary subscribers—who subscribe for love. —If you see Baron d'Holbach, and Diderot, present my respects to them—If the Baron wants any English books, he will let me know, and I will bring them with me—Adieu.

I am truly yours,

L. STERNE.

Letter Ix.

To the same.

London, October 7, 1765.

DEAR SIR,

IT is a terrible thing to be in Paris without a perriwig on a man's head!   In seven days from the date of this, I should be in that case, unless you tell your neighbour Madame Requiere to get her *bon mari de me faire un peruque à bourse, au mieux—c'est-à-dire—une la plus extraordinaire—la plus jolie—la plus gentille—et la plus—*

—Mais qu'importe ? j'ai l'honneur d'être grand critique—et bien difficile encore dans les affaires de peruques —and in one word that he gets it done in five days after notice—

I beg pardon for this liberty, my dear friend, and for the trouble of forwarding this by the very next post.—If my friend Mr F. is in Paris, my kind love to him, and respects to all others—in sad haste—

Yours truly,

L. STERNE.

I have paid into Mr Becket's hands six hundred pounds, which you may draw upon at sight, according as either Mrs Sterne or myself make it expedient.

Letter Ici.

To Mr Panchaud, at Paris.

Beau Point Voisin, November 7, 1765.

DEAR SIR,

I FORGOT to desire you to forward whatever letters came to your hand to your banker at Rome, to wait for me against I get there, as it is uncertain how long I may stay at Turin, &c. &c.; at present I am held prisoner in this town by the sudden swelling of two pitiful rivulets from the snows melting on the Alps—so that we cannot either advance to them, or retire back again to Lyons—for how long the gentlemen who are my fellow-travellers, and myself, shall languish in this state of vexatious captivity, heaven and earth surely know; for it rains as if they were coming together to settle the matter.—I had an agreeable journey to Lyons, and a joyous time there ; dining and supping every day at the commandant's—Lord F. W. I left there, and about a dozen English—If you see Lord Ossory, Lord William Gordon, and my friend Mr Crawford, remember me to them—if Wilkes is at Paris yet, I send him all kind wishes—present my compliments as well as thanks to my good friend Miss P——, and believe me, dear Sir, with all truth, yours,

L. STERNE.

Letter lxij.

To the same.

Turin, November 15, 1765.

Dear Sir,

AFTER many difficulties I have got here safe and sound
—tho' eight days in passing the mountains of Savoy.
—I am stopped here for ten days by the whole country
betwixt here and Milan being laid under water by
continual rains—but I am very happy, and have found
my way into a dozen houses already—To-morrow I
am to be presented to the King, and when that ceremony is over, I shall have my hands full of engage-
ments—No English here but Sir James Macdonald,
who meets with much respect, and Mr Ogilby. We
are all together, and shall depart in peace together——
My kind services to all—pray forward the inclosed—

Yours most truly,
L. Sterne.

Letter lxiij.

To the same.

Turin, November 28, 1765.

Dear Sir,

I AM just leaving this place with Sir James Macdonald
for Milan, &c.—We have spent a joyous fortnight
here, and met with all kinds of honours—and with
regret do we both bid adieu—but health on my side—
and good sense on his—say 'tis better to be at Rome
—you say at Paris—but you put variety out of the
question.—I intreat you to forward the inclosed to

Mrs Sterne—My compliments to all friends, more particularly to those I most value (that includes Mr F. if he is in Paris).

I am yours most truly,

L. STERNE.

Letter LXIV.

To the same.

DEAR SIR, Florence, December 18, 1765.

I HAVE been a month passing the plains of Lombardy —stopping in my way at Milan, Parma, Placenza, and Bologna—with weather as delicious as a kindly April in England, and have been three days in crossing a part of the Apennines covered with thick snow—Sad transition!—I stay here three days to dine with our Plenipo Lords T——d and C——r, and in five days shall tread the Vatican, and be introduced to all the Saints in the Pantheon.—I stay but fourteen days to pay these civilities, and then decamp for Naples.—Pray send the inclosed to my wife, and Becket's letter to London.

Yours truly,

L. STERNE.

Letter LXV.

To Miss Sterne.

MY DEAR GIRL, Naples, February 3, 1766.

YOUR letter, my Lydia, has made me both laugh and cry.—Sorry am I that you are both so afflicted with the ague, and by all means **I wish you both** to fly from Tours, because I remember **it is situated between** two **rivers,** la **Loire,** and le Cher—which must occasion **fogs,** and damp unwholesome weather—therefore for the same reason go **not to** Bourges en Bresse—'tis as **vile a** place **for** agues.—I find myself infinitely better than I was—and hope **to** have added at least ten years to my **life by** this journey to Italy—the climate **is** heavenly, **and** I find new principles of health in **me,** which I **have** been long a stranger to—but **trust me,** my Lydia, I will find you out, wherever you are, in May. Therefore I beg you to direct **to** me at Belloni's at Rome, that I may have some idea where **you** will be then.—The account you **give** me of Mrs C——— **is** truly amiable, I shall ever honour **her—Mr C. is** a diverting companion—what he said of your little French admirer was truly droll—the Marquis de ——— is an impostor, and **not worthy of your** acquaintance—he only **pre-**tended **to know** me, **to** get introduced to your mother —I desire you will get **your** mother to write to Mr C. **that** I may discharge every debt, and then, my Lydia, **if I** live, the produce of my pen shall be yours—If fate **reserves me** not that—the humane and good, part for thy father's sake, part for thy own, will never abandon thee !—If your mother's health will permit her to return with me to England, **your** summers I will **render as** agreeable as I **can at** Coxwould—your winters **at** York —you know **my** publications call **me to** London.—If Mr and Mrs **C—** are still at Tours, thank them from me for **their** cordiality to my wife and daughter. I have purchased **you some** little trifles, which I shall give you when we meet, **as proofs** of affection from

Your fond father,

L. STERNE.

Letter lxvi.

To J— H— S—, Esq.

Naples, February 5, 1766.

My DEAR H.,

'Tis an age since I have heard from you—but as I read the London Chronicle, and find no tidings of your death, or that you are even at the point of it, I take it, as I wish it, that you have got over thus much of the winter free from the damps, both of climate and spirits; and here I am, as happy as a king after all, growing fat, sleek, and well liking—not improving in stature, but in breadth.—We have a jolly carnival of it—nothing but operas—punchinelloes—festinoes and masquerades—We (that is, *nous autres*) are all dressing out for one this night at the Princess Francavivalla, which is to be superb.—The English dine with her (exclusive); and so much for small chat—except that I saw a little comedy acted last week with more expression and spirit, and true character, than I shall see one hastily again.—I stay here till the holy week, which I shall pass at Rome, where I occupy myself a month—My plan was to have gone from thence for a fortnight to Florence—and then by Leghorn to Marseilles directly home—but am diverted from this by the repeated proposals of accompanying a gentleman, who is returning by Venice, Vienna, Saxony, Berlin, and so by the Spaw, and thence through Holland to England—'tis with Mr E. I have known him these three years, and have been with him ever since I reach'd Rome; and as I know him to be a good-hearted young gentleman, I have no doubt of making it answer both his views and mine—at least I am persuaded we shall return home together, as we set out, with friendship and good-will.—Write your next letter to me at Rome, and do me the following favour if it lies in your way, which I think it does—to get me a letter of recommendation to our Ambassador (Lord Stormont at Vienna). I have not the honour to be known to his Lordship, but Lords P—— or H——, or twenty you better know, would write a certificate for me, importing, that I am not fallen out of the clouds. If this will cost my cousin little trouble, do inclose it in your next letter to me at Belloni.—You have left Skelton I trow a month, and I fear have had a most sharp winter, if one may judge of it from the severity of the weather here, and all over Italy, which exceeded any thing known till within these three weeks, that the sun has been as hot as we could bear it.—Give my kind services to my friends—especially to the household of faith—my dear Garland —to Gilbert—to the worthy Colonel—to Cardinal S——, to my fellow-labourer Pantagruel—dear cousin Antony, receive my kindest love and wishes.

Yours affectionately,
L. STERNE.

P.S.—Upon second thoughts, direct your next to me at Mr W., banker at Venice.

Letter lxvij.

To Mr Foley, at Paris.

Naples, February 8, 1766.

DEAR SIR,

I DESIRE Mrs Sterne may have what cash she wants —if she has not received it before now: she sends me word she has been in want of cash these three weeks—be so kind as to prevent this uneasiness to her—which is doubly so to me.—I have made very little use of your letters of credit, having since I left Paris taken up no more money than about fifty louis at Turin, as much at Rome—and a few ducats here—and as I now travel from hence to Rome, Venice, through Vienna to Berlin, &c., with a gentleman of fortune, I shall draw for little more till my return—so you will have always enough to spare for my wife.—The beginning of March be so kind as to let her have a hundred pounds to begin her year with—

There are a good many English here, very few in Rome, or other parts of Italy.—The air of Naples agrees very well with me—I shall return fat—my friendship to all who honour me with theirs—Adieu, my dear friend—I am ever yours,

L. STERNE.

Letter lxviij.

To Mr Panchaud, at Paris.

DEAR SIR,   Naples, February 14, 1766.

I WROTE last week to you, to desire you would let Mrs Sterne have what money she wanted—it may happen, as that letter went inclosed in one to her at Tours, that you will receive this first—I have made little use of your letters of credit, as you will see by that letter, nor shall I want much (if any) till you see me, as I travel now in company with a gentleman — however, as we return by Venice, Vienna, Berlin, &c., to the Spaw, I should be glad if you will draw me a letter of credit upon some one at Venice, to the extent of fifty louis—but I am persuaded I shall not want half of them—however, in

case of sickness or accidents, one would not go so
long a route without money in one's pocket.—The
bankers here are not so conscientious as my friend P. ;
they would make me pay twelve per cent. if I was
to get a letter here.—I beg your letters, &c., may be
inclosed to Mr Watson at Venice—where we shall
be in the Ascension—I have received much benefit
from the air of Naples—but quit it to be at Rome
before the holy week.—There are about five-and-
twenty English here—but most of them will be decamp'd in two months—there are scarce a third of
the number at Rome—I suppose therefore that Paris
is full—my warmest wishes attend you—with my
love to Mr F. and compliments to all—I am, dear
Sir, very faithfully,

Yours,

L. STERNE.

Sir James Macdonald is in the house with me,
and is just recovering a long and most cruel fit of the
rheumatism.

———

Letter lxix.

To J— H— S—, Esq.

DEAR ANTONY,   May 25, near Dijon [1766].

MY desire of seeing both my wife and girl has turn'd
me out of my road towards a delicious Chateau of
the Countess of M————, where I have been pat-
riarching it these seven days with her ladyship, and
half a dozen of very handsome and agreeable ladies
—her ladyship has the best of hearts—a valuable
present not given to every one. To-morrow, with
regret, I shall quit this agreeable circle, and post it

night and day to Paris, where I shall arrive in two days, and just wind myself up, when I am there, enough to roll on to Calais—so I hope to sup with you the king's birth-day, according to a plan of sixteen days standing.—Never man has been such a wildgoose chace after a wife as I have been—after having sought her in five or six different towns, I found her at last in *Franche Compté*—Poor woman! she was very cordial, &c., and begs to stay another year or so—my Lydia pleases me much—I found her greatly improved in every thing I wished her—I am most unaccountably well, and most unaccountably nonsensical—'tis at least a proof of good spirits, which is a sign and token given me in these latter days, that I must take up again the pen—In faith, I think I shall die with it in my hand, but I shall live these ten years, my Antony, notwithstanding the fears of my wife, whom I left most melancholy on that account. This is a delicious part of the world; most celestial weather, and we lie all day, without damps, upon the grass— and that is the whole of it, except the inner man (for her ladyship is not stingy of her wine) is inspired twice a day with the best Burgundy that grows upon the mountains which terminate our lands here.—Surely you will not have decamped to Crazy Castle before I reach town—The summer here is set in in good earnest—'tis more than we can say for Yorkshire— I hope to hear a good tale of your alum-works— have you no other works in hand? I do not expect to hear from you, so God prosper you—and all your undertakings.—I am, my dear cousin,

Most affectionately yours,

L. Sterne.

Remember me to Mr G——, Cardinal S——, the Col., &c. &c. &c.

Letter lɼɼ.

To Mr *Panchaud*, at *Paris.*

York, June **28**, 1766.

DEAR SIR,

I WROTE last **week to** Mr Becket to discharge the balance due to you—and I have received a letter from him, telling me, that if you will draw upon him for one hundred and **sixty** pounds, he will punctually pay it **to** your order—so send the draughts when you please.— Mrs Sterne writes me word, she wants fifty pounds— **which I** desire you will let her have.—I will·take care **to remit** it **to** your correspondent—I **have such** an entire confidence in my wife, that she **spends as** little **as she can,** though she is confined **to no particular** sum —her expenses will **not exceed three hundred** pounds **a year,** unless **by ill health, or a** journey—and **I am** very willing she **should have** it—and **you** may rely, in case it ever happens **that she** should **draw** for fifty or a hundred pounds extraordinary, that it **and** every demand shall be punctually paid—and with proper thanks ; and for this the whole Shandean family are ready to **stand** security.—'Tis impossible to tell you how sorry I was that my affairs hurried me so quick through Paris, as to deprive me of seeing my old friend Mr Foley, and of the pleasure I proposed in being made known **to his** better half—but I have a probability of seeing him this winter.—Adieu, dear **Sir,** and believe me

Most cordially yours,
L. STERNE.

P.S.—Mrs Sterne is going to Chalons, but your letter will **find** her, I believe, at Avignon—She is very poorly—and my daughter writes to me, with sad grief of heart, that she is worse.

Letter lxxi.

To Mr S.

Coxwould, July 23, 1766.

Dear Sir,

One might be led to think that there is a fatality regarding us—we make appointments to meet, and for these two years have not seen each other's face but twice—we must try, and do better for the future—Having sought you with more zeal, than C . . . . sought the Lord, in order to deliver you the books you bade me purchase for you at Paris—I was forced to pay carriage for them from London down to York—but as I shall neither charge you the books nor the carriage—'tis not worth talking about.—Never man, my dear Sir, has had a more agreeable tour than your Yorick—and at present I am in my peaceful retreat, writing the ninth volume * of Tristram—I shall publish but one this year, and the next I shall begin a new work of four volumes, which when finished, I shall continue Tristram with fresh spirit. What a difference of scene here ! But, with a disposition to be happy, 'tis neither this place, nor t'other, that renders us the reverse.—In short, each man's happiness depends upon himself—he is a fool if he does not enjoy it.

What are you about, dear S——? Give me some account of your pleasures—you had better come to me for a fortnight, and I will shew, or give you (if needful), a practical dose of my philosophy; but I hope you do not want it—if you did—'twould be the office of a friend to give it—Will not even our races tempt you? You see I use all arguments—Believe me yours most truly,

Laurence Sterne.

* Alluding to the first edition.

Letter lxxij.

To Mr Panchaud, at Paris.

Coxwould, September 21, 1766.

My dear Friend,

If Mrs Sterne should **draw** upon you for fifty louis d'ors, be **so** kind as to remit her the money—and **pray** be **so** good **as not** to draw upon Mr Becket for **it** (as he owes me nothing), but favour me with the draught, **which** I will pay to Mr Selwin.——A young nobleman **is now** negociating a jaunt with me for six weeks, about Christmas, to the Fauxbourg de **St** Germain—I should like much to be with you for **so** long—and if **my wife** should grow worse (having **had a very** poor account of her in my daughter's last), I **cannot** think of **her** being without me—and however expensive the journey would be, I would fly to Avignon to administer consolation to **both her and my poor girl!—Wherever** I am, believe me, **dear Sir,**

Yours,

L. Sterne.

My kind compliments to **Mr** Foley: though I have not the honour of knowing his rib, I see no reason why I may not present all due respects to the better half of so old a friend, which I do by these presents—with my friendliest wishes **to** Miss P.

Letter lxxiij.

To Mr Foley, at Paris.

Coxwould, October 25, 1766.

My dear Foley,

I desired you would be so good as to remit to Mrs Sterne fifty louis, a month ago—I dare say you have done it—but her illness must have cost her a good deal—therefore having paid the last fifty pounds into Mr Selwin's hands, I beg you to send her thirty guineas more—for which I send a bank bill to Mr Becket by this post—but surely had I not done so, you would not stick at it—for be assured, my dear Foley, that the First Lord of the Treasury is neither more able or more willing (nor perhaps half so punctual) in repaying with honour all I ever can be in your books.—My daughter says her mother is very ill—and I fear going fast down by all accounts—'tis melancholy in her situation to want any aid that is in my power to give—do write to her—and believe me, with all compliments to your Hotel,

Yours very truly,
L. Sterne.

Letter lxxiv.

To Mr Panchaud.

York, November 25, 1766.

Dear Sir,

I just received yours—and am glad that the balance of accounts is now paid to you — Thus far all goes well—I have received a letter from my

daughter with the pleasing tidings that she thinks her
mother out of danger—and that the air of the country
is delightful (excepting the winds) ; but the description of the Chateau my wife has hired is really pretty
—on the side of the Fountain of Vaucluse—with
seven rooms of a floor, half furnished with tapestry,
half with blue taffety, the permission to fish, and to
have game ; so many partridges a week, &c. ; and the
price—guess ! sixteen guineas a year—there's for you,
P.   About the latter end of next month, my wife will
have occasion for a hundred guineas—and pray be so
good, my dear Sir, as to give orders that she may not
be disappointed—she is going to spend the Carnival
at Marseilles at Christmas—I shall be in London by
Christmas week, and then shall balance this remittance
to Mrs S. with Mr S——.   I am going to lie-in of
another child of the Shandaick procreation, in town
—I hope you wish me a safe delivery——I fear my
friend Mr F. will have left town before I get there
—Adieu, dear Sir—I wish you every thing in this
world which will do you good, for I am with unfeigned truth,

Yours,

L. STERNE.

Make my compliments acceptable to the good and
worthy Baron d'Holbach—Miss P., &c. &c.

Letter lxxv.

From Ignatius Sancho, to Mr Sterne.

R<small>EVEREND</small> S<small>IR</small>,   [1766.]

I<small>T</small> would be an insult on your humanity (or perhaps
look like it) to apologize for the liberty I am taking
—I am one of those people whom the vulgar and
illiberal call negroes.—The first part of my life was
rather unlucky, as I was placed in a family who
judged ignorance the best and only security for obedi-
ence.—A little reading and writing I got by un-
wearied application.—The latter part of my life has
been, thro' God's blessing, truly fortunate—having
spent it in the service of one of the best and greatest
families in the kingdom—my chief pleasure has been
books — Philanthropy I adore — How very much,
good Sir, am I (amongst millions) indebted to you
for the character of your amiable Uncle Toby!—I declare I would walk ten miles in the dog-days, to shake
hands with the honest Corporal.—Your sermons have
touch'd me to the heart, and I hope have amended it,
which brings me to the point—In your tenth discourse,* is this very affecting passage—"Consider
how great a part of our species in all ages down to
this—have been trod under the feet of cruel and cap-
ricious tyrants, who would neither hear their cries,
nor pity their distresses.—Consider slavery—what it
is—how bitter a draught—and how many millions are
made to drink of it."—Of all my favourite authors,
not one has drawn a tear in favour of my miserable
black brethren—excepting yourself, and the humane
author of Sir Geo. Ellison.—I think you will forgive me; I am sure you will applaud me for beseeching

* *I.e.*, Sermon x. on Job.

L.   I

you to give one half-hour's attention to slavery, as
it is this day practised in our West Indies.—That
subject handled in your striking manner would ease
the yoke (perhaps) of many—but if only of one—
gracious God! what a feast to a benevolent heart!
and sure I am, you are an epicurean in acts of charity.
—You who are universally read, and as universally
admired—you could not fail.—Dear Sir, think in me
you behold the uplifted hands of thousands of my
brother Moors. Grief (you pathetically observe) is
eloquent: figure to yourself their attitudes; hear their
supplicating addresses!—alas! you cannot refuse.—
Humanity must comply—in which hope I beg permission to subscribe myself,

Reverend Sir, &c.,

I. S.

Letter lrrbl.

From Mr Sterne, to Ignatius Sancho.

Coxwould, July 27, 1766.

THERE is a strange coincidence, Sancho, in the little
events (as well as in the great ones) of this world: for
I had been writing a tender tale of the sorrows of
a friendless poor negro-girl, and my eyes had scarce
done smarting with it, when your letter of recommendation, in behalf of so many of her brethren and
sisters, came to me—but why *her brethren?* or yours,
Sancho! any more than mine? It is by the finest
tints, and most insensible gradations, that nature de-
scends from the fairest face about St James's, to the
sootiest complexion in Africa:—at which tint of these
is it, that the ties of blood are to cease? and how

many shades must we descend lower still in the scale, ere mercy is to vanish with them? But 'tis no uncommon thing, my good Sancho, for one half of the world to use the other half of it like brutes, and then endeavour to make 'em so.—For my own part, I never look *westward* (when I am in a pensive mood at least) but I think of the burthens which our brothers and sisters are *there* carrying, and could I ease their shoulders from one ounce of them, I declare I would set out this hour upon a pilgrimage to Mecca for their sakes—which by the bye, Sancho, exceeds your walk of ten miles in about the same proportion that a visit of humanity should one of mere form.—However, if you meant my Uncle Toby, more he is your debtor.— If I can weave the tale I have wrote into the work I am about—'tis at the service of the afflicted—and a much greater matter; for in serious truth, it casts a sad shade upon the world, that so great a part of it are, and have been so long bound in chains of darkness, and in chains of misery; and I cannot but both respect and felicitate you, that by so much laudable diligence you have broke the one—and that by falling into the hands of so good and merciful a family, Providence has rescued you from the other.

And so, good-hearted Sancho, adieu! and believe me I will not forget your letter.

Yours,

L. STERNE.

Letter lxxbij.

To Mr W.

Coxwould, December 20, 1766.

THANKS, my dear **W.**, for your letter.—I am just preparing to **come** and greet you and many other friends in town—I **have** drained my ink-standish to the bottom, and after I have published, shall set my face, not **towards** Jerusalem, but towards **the** Alps—I find I **must** once more fly from death whilst **I** have strength —I shall go to Naples, and see whether the air of that place will not set this poor frame to rights—As **to** the project of getting **a bear** to lead, I think **I** have enough **to** do to govern myself—and however profitable it might be (according **to** your opinion), I am sure it would be unpleasurable—Few are the **minutes** of life, **and I do not think that I** have any to **throw away on** any one being.——I shall spend nine or ten months in Italy, and call upon my wife **and** daughter in France at my return—so shall be back by the King's birth-day —what a project!—And now, my dear friend, am I going to York, not for the sake of society—nor to walk by the side of the muddy Ouse, but to recruit myself of the most violent spitting of blood that **ever** mortal man experienced ; because I had **rather (in case 'tis** ordained **so)** die there, **than in a post-chaise on** the road.—If the a[r]mour of my **Uncle** Toby do not **please you, I am** mistaken—and **so with a** droll story I **will finish this** letter—A sensible **friend** of mine, with **whom, not** long ago, I spent **some** hours in conversa**tion,** met an apothecary (an acquaintance of ours)—the latter asked him how he **did** ? why, ill, very ill—I have been with Sterne, who **has** given me such a dose of *Attic salt* that I am in a fever—Attic **salt,** Sir,

Attic salt! I have Glauber salt,—I have Epsom salt
in my shop, &c.—Oh! I suppose 'tis some French
salt—I wonder you would trust his report of the
medicine, he cares not what he takes himself—I fancy
I see you smile—I long to be able to be in London,
and embrace my friends there—and shall enjoy myself
a week or ten days at Paris with my friends, particularly the Baron d'Holbach, and the rest of the joyous
sett—As to the females—no, I will not say a word
about them—only I hate borrowed characters taken up
(as a woman does her shift) for the purpose she intends
to effectuate.   Adieu, adieu—I am yours whilst

L. Sterne.

Letter Ixxbiij.

To Mr Panchaud, at Paris.

Dear P.,   London, February 13, 1767.

I paid yesterday (by Mr Becket) a hundred guineas,
or pounds, I forget which, to Mr Selwin—But you
must remit to Mrs Sterne at Marseilles a hundred
louis before she leaves that place, which will be in less
than three weeks.   Have you got the ninth volume of
Shandy?*—'tis liked the best of all here.—I am going
to publish a Sentimental Journey through France and
Italy—the undertaking is protected and highly en-
couraged by all our noblesse—'tis subscribed for, at a
great rate—'twill be an original—in large quarto—the
subscription half a guinea—If you can procure me the
honour of a few names of men of science, or fashion, I
shall thank you—they will appear in good company, as

---

* Alluding to the first edition.

all the nobility here almost have honoured me with their names.——My kindest remembrance to Mr Foley —respects to Baron d'Holbach, **and believe me ever** ever yours,

L. STERNE.

Letter lxxix.

To Miss **Sterne.**

Old Bond-street, February **23**, 1767.

AND so, my Lydia! thy mother **and** thyself are returning back again from Marseilles **to the** banks of the Sorgue—and there thou wilt sit and fish for trouts—I envy you the sweet situation.——Petrarch's tomb I should like to **pay a** sentimental visit to——the Fountain of Vaucluse, **by thy** description, must **be** delightful—I am **also much pleased** with the account you give me of the **Abbé de** Sade—you find great comfort in such a neigh-**bour—I am** glad he is so good as to correct thy translation **of** my Sermons—dear girl, go on, and make me a present of thy work—but why not the House of Mourning? 'tis one of the best. I long to receive the life of Petrarch, and his Laura, by your Abbé; **but I am out of** all patience with the answer the Marquis **made the** Abbé—'twas truly coarse, and I wonder he **bore it with any** Christian patience—But **to the** subject **of** your letter—I do not wish **to know** who was the busy fool, who made your mother uneasy about Mrs ———; 'tis true I have a friendship for her, but not to infatuation—I believe I **have** judgment enough to discern hers, and every woman's faults. I honour thy mother for her answer—"that she wished **not** to be informed, **and** begged him **to** drop the subject."——

Why do you say that your mother wants money?—whilst I have a shilling, shall you not both have nine-pence out of it?—I think, if I have my enjoyments, I ought not to grudge you yours.—I shall not begin my Sentimental Journey till I get to Coxwould—I have laid a plan for something new, quite out of the beaten track.—I wish I had you with me—and I would introduce you to one of the most amiable and gentlest of beings, whom I have just been with—not Mrs ————, but a Mrs J., the wife of as worthy a man as I ever met with—I esteem them both. He possesses every manly virtue—honour and bravery are his charac-teristics, which have distinguished him nobly in several instances—I shall make you better acquainted with his character, by sending Orme's History, with the books you desired—and it is well worth your reading; for Orme is an elegant writer, and a just one; he pays no man a compliment at the expence of truth.—Mrs J—— is kind,—and friendly—of a sentimental turn of mind—and so sweet a disposition, that she is too good for the world she lives in—Just God! if all were like her, what a life would this be!—Heaven, my Lydia, for some wise purpose has created different beings—I wish my dear child knew her—thou art worthy of her friendship, and she already loves thee; for I sometimes tell her what I feel for thee.—This is a long letter—write soon, and never let your letters be studied ones—write naturally, and then you will write well.—I hope your mother has got quite well of her ague—I have sent her some of Huxham's tincture of the Bark.—I will order you a guittar, since the other is broke. Be-lieve me, my Lydia, that I am yours affectionately,

L. STERNE.

Letter lxxx.

To Mr Panchaud, at Paris.

London, February 27, 1767.

Dear Sir,

My daughter begs a present of me, and you must know I can deny her nothing—It must be strung with catgut, and of five cords—*sic hiama in Italiano la chitera di cinque corde*—she cannot get such a thing at Marseilles—at Paris one may have every thing—Will you be so good to my girl as to make her happy in this affair, by getting some musical body to buy one, and send it her to Avignon directed to Monsieur Teste?—I wrote last week to desire you would remit Mrs S. a hundred louis—'twill be all, except the guittar, I shall owe you—send me your account, and I will pay Mr Selwin—direct to me at Mr Becket's—all kind respects to my friend Mr F. and your sister.

Yours cordially,
L. Sterne.

Letter lxxxi.*

To Eliza.†

Eliza will receive my books with this. The sermons came all hot from the heart: I wish that I could give them any title to be offered to yours.—The others

* This and the nine following Letters have no dates to them, but were evidently written in the months of March and April 1767. They are therefore here placed together.

† The Editor of the first publication of Mr Sterne's Letters to Eliza gives the following account of this lady: "Mrs Elizabeth Draper, wife of Daniel Draper, Esq., counsellor at Bombay, and at present (*i.e.*, in 1775) chief of the factory at Surat, a gentleman very much respected in that quarter of the globe.—

came from the head—I am more indifferent about their reception.

I know not how it comes about, but I am half in love with you—I ought to be wholly so; for I never valued (or saw more good qualities to value) or thought more of one of your sex than of you; so adieu.

Yours faithfully,

If not affectionately,

L. STERNE.

She is by birth an East Indian; but the circumstance of being born in the country, not proving sufficient to defend her delicate frame against the heats of that burning climate, she came to England for the recovery of her health, when by accident she became acquainted with Mr Sterne. He immediately discovered in her a mind so congenial with his own, so enlightened, so refined, and so tender, that their mutual attraction presently joined them in the closest union that purity could possibly admit of: he loved her as his friend, and prided in her as his pupil; all her concerns became presently his; her health, her circumstances, her reputation, her children, were his; his fortune, his time, his country, were at her disposal, so far as the sacrifice of all or any of these might, in his opinion, contribute to her real happiness. If it is asked, whether the glowing heat of Mr Sterne's affection never transported him to a flight beyond the limits of pure Platonism, the publisher will not take upon him absolutely to deny it; but this he thinks, so far from leaving any stain upon that gentleman's memory, that it perhaps includes his fairest encomium; since to cherish the seeds of piety and chastity in a heart which the passions are interested to corrupt, must be allowed to be the noblest effort of a soul fraught and fortified with the justest sentiments of religion and virtue."

After reading these letters, the curiosity of the public will be naturally excited to enquire concerning the fate of the lady to whom they were addressed. To this question it will be sufficient to answer, that she hath been dead some years, and that it might give pain to many worthy persons if the circumstances which attended the latter part of her life were disclosed, as they are generally said to have reflected no credit either on her prudence or discretion.

Letter lxxxij.

To the same.

I CANNOT rest, Eliza, though I shall call on you at half-
past twelve, till I know how you do—May **thy** dear
face smile, as **thou** risest, like the sun of this morning.
I was much grieved to hear of your alarming indisposi-
tion yesterday ; **and** disappointed too, at not being let
in.—Remember, my dear, that a friend has the same
right as a physician. The etiquettes of this town
(**you'll** say) say otherwise.—No matter ! Delicacy
and propriety do not always consist in observing their
frigid doctrines.

I am going out to breakfast, but **shall be at** my
lodgings by eleven ; when I hope to **read a** single line
under thy own hand, that thou art better, and wilt be
glad to see **thy** Bramin.

9 o'clock.

Letter lxxxiij.

To the same.

I GOT thy letter last night, Eliza, on my return from
Lord Bathurst's, where I dined, and where **I was** heard
(as I talked of thee **an** hour without intermission)
with so much pleasure and attention, that **the** good
old Lord **toasted** your health three different times ;
and now he is in his eighty-fifth year, says he hopes
to live long enough **to** be introduced as a friend to my
fair Indian disciple, and to **see** her eclipse all other
nabobesses as much in wealth, **as** she does already in
exterior and (what is far better) in interior **merit.** I

hope so too. This nobleman is an old friend of mine. —You know he was always the protector of men of wit and genius ; and has had those of the last century, Addison, Steele, Pope, Swift, Prior, &c. &c., always at his table.—The manner in which his notice began of me, was as singular as it was polite.—He came up to me, one day, as I was at the Princess of Wales's court. "I want to know you, Mr Sterne ; but it is fit you should know, also, who it is that wishes this pleasure. You have heard, continued he, of an old Lord Bathurst, of whom your Popes and Swifts have sung and spoken so much : I have lived my life with geniuses of that cast ; but have survived them ; and, despairing ever to find their equals, it is some years since I have closed my accounts, and shut up my books, with thoughts of never opening them again ; but you have kindled a desire in me of opening them once more before I die ; which I now do ; so go home and dine with me."—This nobleman, I say, is a prodigy ; for at eighty-five he has all the wit and promptness of a man of thirty. A disposition to be pleased, and a power to please others beyond whatever I knew : added to which, a man of learning, courtesy, and feeling.

He heard me talk of thee, Eliza, with uncommon satisfaction ;—for there was only a third person, and of sensibility, with us.—And a most sentimental afternoon, till nine o'clock, have we passed ! But thou, Eliza, wert the star that conducted and enliven'd the discourse.—And when I talked not of thee, still didst thou fill my mind, and warmed every thought I uttered, for I am not ashamed to acknowledge I greatly miss thee.—Best of all good girls ! the sufferings I have sustained the whole night on account of thine, Eliza, are beyond my power of words.—Assuredly does Heaven give strength proportioned to the weight he lays upon us! Thou hast **been bowed** down, my **child, with every** burden that sorrow **of** heart, and **pain of** body, could inflict upon **a** poor being; and still thou tellest me, thou **art** beginning to get ease;— **thy** fever gone, thy sickness, the pain in **thy** side vanishing also.—May every evil so vanish that **thwarts** Eliza's happiness, or **but** awakens thy fears **for a** moment!— Fear nothing, **my** dear!— Hope **every** thing; and the balm of this passion will shed its **in**-fluence on thy health, and make thee enjoy a spring of youth and cheerfulness, more than thou hast hardly yet **tasted.**

And so thou hast fixed thy Bramin's portrait over thy writing-desk; and wilt consult it in all doubts and difficulties.——Grateful and good girl! Yorick smiles contentedly over all thou dost; his picture **does not** do **justice to** his own complacency.

Thy sweet little plan and distribution **of thy** time— **how** worthy of thee! Indeed, Eliza, thou leavest me nothing to direct **thee in; thou** leavest me nothing to require, nothing to ask—but a continuation of that conduct which won my esteem, and has made me thy friend for **ever.**

May the roses come quick **back** to thy cheeks, and the rubies to thy lips! But trust my declaration, Eliza, that thy husband (if he is the good, feeling man I wish him) will press thee to him with more honest warmth and affection, and kiss thy pale, poor dejected face, with more transport, than he would be able to do, in the **best** bloom of all thy beauty;—and **so he** ought, or I pity him. He must have strange feelings, if he **knows not** the value of such a creature as thou art!

I am glad Miss Light* goes with you. She may

---

* Miss Light afterwards married George Stratton, Esq., late in the service of the East-India Company at Madras. She is since dead.

relieve you from many anxious moments.—I am glad your ship-mates are friendly beings. You could least dispense with what is contrary to your own nature, which is soft and gentle, Eliza.—It would civilize savages.—Though pity were it thou shouldst be tainted with the office! How canst thou make apologies for thy last letter? 'tis most delicious to me, for the very reason you excuse it. Write to me, my child, only such. Let them speak the easy carelessness of a heart that opens itself, any how, and every how, to a man you ought to esteem and trust. Such, Eliza, I write to thee,—and so I should ever live with thee, most art- lessly, most affectionately, if Providence permitted thy residence in the same section of the globe :—for I am, all that honour and affection can make me,

THY BRAMIN.

Letter lxxxix.

To the same.

I WRITE this, Eliza, at Mr James's, whilst he is dress- ing, and the dear girl, his wife, is writing, beside me, to thee.—I got your melancholy billet before we sat down to dinner. 'Tis melancholy indeed, my dear, to hear so piteous an account of thy sickness! Thou art encountered with evils enow, without that additional weight! I fear it will sink thy poor soul, and body with it, past recovery—Heaven supply thee with forti- tude! We have talked of nothing but thee, Eliza, and of thy sweet virtues, and endearing conduct, all the afternoon. Mrs James, and thy Bramin, have mixed their tears a hundred times, in speaking of thy hardships, thy goodness, thy graces.—The ****'s by heavens, are worthless! I have heard enough to tremble at the articulation of the name.—How could you, Eliza, leave them (or suffer them to leave you rather) with impressions the least favourable? I have told thee enough to plant disgust against their treachery to thee, to the last hour of thy life! Yet still thou toldest Mrs James at last, that thou believest they affectionately love thee.—Her delicacy to my Eliza, and true regard to her ease of mind, have saved thee from hearing more glaring proofs of their baseness— For God's sake, write not to them; nor foul thy fair character with such polluted hearts—*They* love thee! What proof? Is it their actions that say so? or their zeal for those attachments, which do thee honour, and make thee happy? or their tenderness for thy fame? No—But they *weep* and say *tender things.*—Adieu to all such for ever. Mrs James's honest heart revolts against the idea of ever returning them one visit.—I honour her, and I honour thee, for almost every act of thy life, but this blind partiality for an unworthy being.

Forgive my zeal, dear girl, and allow me a right which arises only out of that fund of affection I have, and shall preserve for thee to the hour of my death! Reflect, Eliza, what are my motives for perpetually advising thee? think whether I can have any, but what proceed from the cause I have mentioned! I think you are a very deserving woman; and that you want nothing but firmness and a better opinion of your-self to be the best female character I know. I wish I could inspire you with a share of that vanity your enemies lay to your charge (though to me it has never been visible); because I think, in a well-turned mind, it will produce good effects.

I probably shall never see you more; yet I flatter myself you'll sometimes think of me with pleasure; because you must be convinced I love you, and so interest myself in your rectitude, that I had rather hear of any evil befalling you, than your want of reverence for yourself. I had not power to keep this remonstrance in my breast.—It's now out; so adieu. Heaven watch over my Eliza!

Thine,

Yorick.

Letter lxxxb.

To the same.

To whom should Eliza apply in her distress, but to her friend who loves her? why then, my dear, do you apologize for employing me? Yorick would be offended, and with reason, if you ever sent commissions to another, which he could execute. I have been with Zumps; and your piano forté must be tuned from the brass middle string of your guittar, which is C.— I have got you a hammer too, and a pair of plyers to twist your wire with; and may every one of them, my dear, vibrate sweet comfort to my hopes! I have bought you ten handsome brass screws, to hang your necessaries upon: I purchased twelve; but stole a couple from you to put up in my own cabin, at Coxwould—I shall never hang, or take my hat off one of them, but I shall think of you. I have bought thee, moreover, a couple of iron screws, which are more to be depended on than brass, for the globes.

I have written, also, to Mr Abraham Walker, pilot at Deal, that I had dispatched these in a packet, directed to his care; which I desired he would seek after, the moment the Deal machine arrived. I have, moreover, given him directions, what sort of an arm-chair you would want, and have directed him to purchase the best that Deal could afford, and take it, with the parcel, in the first boat that went off. Would I could, Eliza, so supply all thy wants, and all thy wishes! It would be a state of happiness to me.—The journal is as it should be—all but its contents. Poor, dear, patient being! I do more than pity you; for I think I lose both firmness and philosophy, as I figure to myself your distresses. Do not think I spoke last night with too much asperity of ****; there was cause; and besides, a good heart ought not to love a bad one; and, indeed, cannot. But, adieu to the ungrateful subject.

I have been this morning to see Mrs James—She loves thee tenderly, and unfeignedly.—She is alarmed for thee—She says thou looked'st most ill and melancholy on going away. She pities thee. I shall visit her every Sunday, while I am in town. As this may be my last letter, I earnestly bid thee farewell.—May the God of Kindness be kind to thee, and approve himself thy protector, now thou art defenceless! And, for thy daily comfort, bear in thy mind this truth, that whatever measure of sorrow and distress is thy portion, it will be repaid to thee in a full measure of happiness, by the Being thou hast wisely chosen for thy eternal friend.

Farewell, farewell, Eliza! whilst I live, count upon me as the most warm and disinterested of earthly friends.

YORICK.

END OF VOL. I.

BALLANTYNE PRESS: EDINBURGH AND LONDON

www.ingramcontent.com/pod-product-compliance
Lightning Source LLC
Chambersburg PA
CBHW020013030726

47500CB00002B/560